WELCOME HOME

Welcome Home

SCRIPTURE, PRAYERS, AND BLESSINGS
FOR THE HOUSEHOLD

YEAR OF LUKE

Augsburg Fortress
Minneapolis

WELCOME HOME
Scripture, Prayers, and Blessings for the Household, Year of Luke

Sources of prayers and other seasonal materials are acknowledged on pages 162–165.

Editors: Samuel Torvend, Linda Parriott
Cover design: Lecy Design
Interior design: Marti Naughton
Contributors: Susan Cherwien, Shawn Madigan, Craig Mueller, Gail Ramshaw

The paper used in this publication meets the minimum requirements of American National Standard for Information Sciences—Permanence of Paper for Printed Library Materials, ANSI Z329.48-1984.

Manufactured in the U.S.A.   ISBN 0-8066-3329-8   10-33298
           02   01   00   99   98   97   1   2   3   4   5   6   7   8

Table of Contents

Introduction

How to use this book

INTRODUCTIONS THROUGHOUT THE BOOK

When you have time, read the brief introductions to Daily Prayer and Sunday. These introductions set forth the various possibilities for prayer in the household. At the beginning of each of the nine seasons, a seasonal introduction sets forth the meaning of that time of the year.

THREE PATTERNS OF PRAYER

Daily prayer contains short forms of prayer for use at various times: waking, morning, midday, evening, and going to bed. Though the patterns of prayer presented here begin with morning and end with nighttime, the reader is free to use whatever is helpful given the diverse situations that mark contemporary household life.

For Christians, Sunday is the Lord's Day when the community of faith gathers at the table of the Word of God and the table of the holy supper. From the very beginning, Christians have set this day apart with prayer in the home. This book offers two patterns of *Sunday prayer*, one for the morning and another for the evening.

During the seasons of the year, the daily or Sunday pattern of prayer can be filled with new songs, psalms, and blessings. The pattern of *seasonal prayer* allows the household to experience the church's cycle of feasts and seasons, which offers new images, customs, and cherished household practices. In this book, seasonal prayer begins with Advent (December) and ends with November.

TABLE PRAYER

At mealtime, use the Sunday or seasonal table prayer. Read the seasonal invitation, pause for a moment, and then pray the table prayer. The household is free to expand upon this simple meal blessing by lighting candles, singing a song, or listening to a brief passage from scripture.

SONG

Songs have been included for morning, evening, and bedtime prayer, Sunday, and each season of the year. While the hymn or song may be used at the beginning of prayer, it can be sung or read at any time of the day or season. If you do not know the tune to a hymn (printed below the last verse), use the hymn index in the back of the book. Other tunes are listed there. If more than one person will be singing, it will be helpful to have copies of this book available for group use.

THE PSALMS

For hundreds of years, the psalms have been the prayerbook of Jews and Christians. By praying the psalms, contemporary Christians learn to pray with their spiritual ancestors, with Christ, and with the communion of saints. If you use this book by yourself, slowly pray the psalm silently or out loud. If more than one person prays the psalm, the verses may be prayed alternately. The psalm translations in the book are those of the New Revised Standard Version of the Bible

SCRIPTURE

With each season, the Sunday lectionary readings are printed in this book. In addition to the Sunday readings, a table of daily readings is printed for the week. This list of daily readings is rooted in and expands upon the scripture readings from the previous Sunday. In this way, the images, actions, and words of Sunday flow into the week.

The scripture readings may be read silently for personal reflection or out loud when a group of persons is gathered for prayer. The privilege of reading the Word of God may be shared among those who gather for prayer. After the reading, keep silence for a time so that the words may find a place to dwell in memory and the imagination. Resist the temptation to fill the silence with sound.

SCRIPTURE-RELATED PRAYERS

For each week of the year, two prayers based on the Sunday readings are provided. One is a brief prayer, easily memorized, that can be prayed throughout the day. These short biblical invocations are easily learned by children so that from an early age, the words of scripture become a part of the child's vocabulary. A prayer for use throughout the week offers a brief summary of one of the Sunday readings.

CANTICLE

Since the early centuries of the church, Christians have prayed the Song of Zechariah (the Benedictus) in the morning, the Song of Mary (the Magnificat) in the evening, and the Song of Simeon (the Nunc dimittis) at night or at bedtime. Throughout the world today, millions of Christians sing or recite these central songs of the New Testament in hundreds of different languages. When we use these canticles, we join our voices with those of Christians in distant lands.

In addition to these cherished canticles, this book offers Sunday and seasonal canticles for use in the home. Use the daily or seasonal canticle or alternate between them in longer seasons.

PRAYER

Each pattern—daily, Sunday, and seasonal—provides an opportunity for prayer. Following the pattern of Sunday worship, household prayer moves from personal and/or family concerns to the larger circle of intercession for the community, the nation, and those in particular need. The Lord's Prayer and a seasonal or weekly prayer may conclude the prayers.

BLESSINGS FOR VARIOUS OCCASIONS AND PERSONS

Throughout the seasons, various blessings are included in this book. These blessings are related to household customs (e.g, the lighting of Advent candles), days (e.g., Christmas), or a particular need (e.g., travel). Anyone in the household who is capable of doing so, may read the prayer of blessing. When it is appropriate, the prayer of blessing may be expanded with the singing of a song, reading a passage from scripture, and/or praying the Lord's Prayer.

CALENDAR FOR THE YEAR OF LUKE

The Sunday scripture readings in this book follow the Revised Common Lectionary for Year C in which the Gospels of Luke and John are prominent. In the back of this book, a calendar lists the years and dates in which this cycle of readings will be used in the churches. The seasonal section of this book begins with Advent (December) and continues through November of the next calendar year. This book may be used in these years: 1997–1998, 2000–2001, 2003–2004, 2006–2007, 2009–2010.

Basic Elements of Prayer in the Home

In words and actions, the household can become a spiritual center where faith, hope, and love flourish in good times and in bad. This centeredness does not happen, however, through wishful thinking. Whether one lives alone or with others, it is important to cultivate a simple pattern of daily and seasonal prayer. Christians are intentional about fostering household prayer, not because God needs it or demands it, but because the words and songs, the customs and prayers of the household can lead us to see all of life from the perspective of faith. God has become one with our time, our place, our daily lives through the incarnation of the Son. In the pattern of Jesus' prayer, in his words and gestures, Christians see the way God invites us to live in our time and in our homes.

WHEN WE PRAY

The first Christians, being Jews, followed the patterns of prayer present in their religion and culture. They filled the patterns, however, with the life of Jesus Christ. Thus, since the earliest days, Christians have prayed in *the morning, at midday, in the evening, and at bedtime.* The images of the day—sunrise, noon, sunset, nighttime—became ways to understand the presence of Christ throughout the day. And so Christians speak and sing of Christ the light who never sets, Christ the dawning light of God's mercy.

In the middle of the night, Christ rose from the dead and appeared to his followers on Sunday, the first day of the week: he opened the scriptures to them; he offered them his peace; he broke bread and shared a cup with them; he sent them forth into the world to proclaim the good news in word and act. For Christians, *Sunday is the day of Christ's resurrection* when the people of God gather to hear Christ speak in the scriptures, to celebrate baptism, to receive his peace, and to share his bread and cup with each other.

The center of the Christian year is the *Three Days of Maundy/ Holy Thursday, Good Friday*, and *Holy Saturday/Easter Sunday* during which believers celebrate Christ's passover from suffering and death to risen life. The Easter Vigil/Easter Sunday is the primary baptismal festival of the year. The *Forty Days of Lent* invite the Christian community to examine its faithfulness to God's promises in baptism, to turn away from sin and receive God's mercy. In the *Fifty Days of Easter*, Christians celebrate the presence of the risen Christ and ask what it means to be his followers in public life.

The Christmas season draws our attention to the ever-present Christ who is our Word and our Light. During *Advent*, we prepare to welcome the Light. We listen to the prophets who announce God's reign of justice and peace. During the *Twelve Days of Christmas* we celebrate the presence of the Word-made-flesh who is Emmanuel, God with us. The festival of the *Epiphany* marks Christ's manifestation to the nations of the earth and invites Christians to participate in the church's global outreach. The Baptism of the Lord marks the beginning of Jesus' public ministry.

The many *Sundays after Pentecost* correspond to *Summer* and the first two months of *Autumn.* From the feast of All Saints to Christ the King/Reign of Christ, the Sunday readings during *November* draw us to contemplation of the last things: the communion of saints, the resurrection of the dead, and the life of the world to come.

These many feasts and seasons influence the daily and weekly practice of prayer. They present a rhythm that shapes the Christian awareness of God's presence in all seasons of the year and all seasons of human life. They invite us to celebrate this merciful presence in the many customs of the household.

WHERE WE PRAY

Prayer and reading may take place anywhere in the home: in a bedroom, out in the garden or yard, around the table, in the living room. For many people, a visual focus or place for prayer is important: a cross or crucifix, a burning candle, a sacred image or icon. Throughout the seasons of the year, the place of prayer can vary: around the Advent wreath, close to the Christmas tree, next to a nativity scene, near a cross, around a bowl of water or vase of flowers, in the light of a burning candle.

HOW WE PRAY

We learn the words of faith and their many meanings by speaking them, listening to them, praying them, singing them. We also learn the words of faith by letting them speak in silence: The reading of scripture invites us to be quiet so that we might truly hear the Word speaking within us.

The faithful people of God pray for the needs of the Christian community, the nation and the world, the sick and dying, and the poor and needy. The needs of the day or the particular time in which we live are brought before God. It is that time when we can speak the truth, trusting in God's mercy. In prayers of intercession, some people fold their hands while others open them, palms up.

When we were baptized, the sign of the cross was traced on our foreheads. In some Christian communions, the cross is traced on the lips and the heart as well. Since the earliest centuries, Christians have traced the cross on their foreheads or their bodies when they rise in the morning, at prayer, and when they go to bed at night. It is with this simple gesture that women, men, and children are marked for life at baptism.

Parents may bless their children just as friends may bless each other by placing their two hands on the head of the other person. It is an intimate gesture as old as Abraham and as new as the mother who places her hands on the head of her young child. Such a gesture conveys favor, affection, and love.

Some people kneel as they pray, others stand or sit. Some people pray while walking, running, or working. The simple gestures of everyday life—open arms in welcome, an embrace, a handshake, washing, planting, eating—can be the gestures of pray. The more momentous transitions of life—birth, leaving home, entering school, moving and separation, marriage, sickness, birthdays and reunions, dying and death—can be the opportunities for household prayer.

When going on a retreat, traveling, or visiting the sick and homebound, take this book with you. If you have no words for prayer, let these words speak for you until your voice returns. May *Welcome Home* assist you in the daily, Sunday, and seasonal rhythm of prayer.

The Gospel of Luke

Through the centuries, artists have portrayed Luke as an ox, a physician, and a painter. Some people think Luke's Gospel is symbolized by an ox because oxen were sacrificed at the Temple, a key location in this gospel. Luke's narrative begins in the Temple precinct as the priest Zechariah (John the Baptist's father) prepares to burn incense (1:5-23). The gospel ends as the disciples of the risen Lord return to the Temple, after the ascension, where they bless God day after day (24:52-53). By filling his narrative with many references to the Temple—the central sacred place of Jewish faith—Luke uses this old image as a way of speaking something new about Jesus: for Christians, the crucified and risen Lord is the temple. He is the living, holy shelter stretching across cultures and times to encompass all humanity. To speak of Jesus as the new temple is to suggest that the primary place of God's presence is within human life. Indeed, it is Luke who highlights the silent yet powerful presence of the Holy Spirit in the life of Jesus, the disciples, and the Christian community. In this "gospel of the Holy Spirit, " the reader recognizes that Jesus' followers are drawn into this living temple whose cornerstone is Christ and whose soul is the Spirit.

Luke is quite clear in recognizing that salvation is offered to all people regardless of natural distinctions or the divisions humans have created. There is room in the temple of Christ's body for all sorts of people: Jews and Gentiles, women and men, lepers and rulers, shepherds and soldiers, the elderly and the very young. All are welcome in their great differences. All are washed in the waters of baptism, sloughing off the world's drive to make the remarkable and God-given diversity of life a source of disunity.

The medieval spiritual writer Dante called Luke the "scribe of Christ's gentleness" because of his emphasis on Jesus' mercy for all people, especially the poor, outcasts, and sinners. In this third gospel, the reader can see Jesus in the act of drawing people into the circle of God's mercy. He heals the sick, feeds the hungry, and serves the weak. He announces that the little ones of this earth are blessed with God's favor. In the kingdom of God, all things are turned upside down: a deathly cross becomes the Tree of Life and the powerless are crowned as queens and kings. Indeed, Jesus himself reigns from the throne of the cross, his broken body the sign of God's presence for all who find their lives broken and in need of healing.

As if he were painting a portrait of Jesus' life and ministry, Luke colors his gospel and the Acts of the Apostles with many vivid images. Little wonder that so many of his stories have been adapted as songs, plays, and religious artwork. Imbued with colorful details, the descriptive character of the gospel fills the mind with many images of God's mercy for sinners, the sick, and the troubled people of the earth.

Luke calls his narrative an "orderly account of events," written for his friend Theophilus (i.e., a lover of God). This orderly account is Luke's way of presenting both the human journey from birth to death and Jesus' journey from earth to heaven. And with a careful reading of this gospel, it becomes clear that the human journey is suffused now with the Lord's presence through the Spirit. It is this merciful presence in the small details of life that gives Jesus' followers cause for happiness and rejoicing. Where there is mercy and forgiveness, there is peace and joy. These are not abstract values or vague feelings in the gospel; they have been etched into the lives of those who walk in the presence of the Lord.

Be welcome, then, to this gospel of mercy and pardon. In its words and images, find the way to fashion a house of mercy where you live.

Daily

aily prayer is an essential practice for those who seek to hear God's voice and cultivate an inner life. Whether one prays alone or with others, in simplicity or festive delight, with brevity or sustained meditation, the rhythm of daily prayer reveals the life-sustaining communion to which God invites all human beings. Such prayer is a serene power silently at work, drawing us into the ancient yet vital sources of faith, hope, and love.

Since the earliest days of Christianity, the followers of Jesus have prayed as he did: in the morning, in the evening, and before going to bed. When possible they have prayed, albeit briefly, at midday. This rhythm of prayer follows the daily cycle—sunrise, noon, sunset, nighttime—and allows the Christian community to recognize the living presence of Christ in all times and all places: upon waking to a new day, during the rush of labor, in the darkness of night. "If I climb up to heaven, you are there," writes the psalmist, "if I make the grave my bed, you are there also. If I take the wings of morning and dwell in the uttermost parts of the seas, even there your hand will lead me and your right hand hold me fast" (Psalm 139:7-11).

Our prayer may be nothing more than the simple invocation of Christ's name or the blessing of the Trinity repeated throughout the day. It may include the reading of a psalm or a selection of scripture. We may pray the Lord's Prayer—the model of all Christian prayer—three times a day. When

Prayer

members of a household gather for a meal, both the simple and festive patterns of prayer outlined in this book may be shared among those present.

Even though Christians gather on the Lord's Day—Sunday—for public worship, much of our time is spent in the home. We first learn the words, the gestures, and the songs of faith in the home. We discover our essential identity as a community of faith in the home. We mark the many significant transitions of life—from birth to death—in the home. To surround and infuse the daily rhythm of sleeping and waking, working and resting, bathing and eating with the words and gestures of Christian prayer is to discover the ancient truth of the gospel: the ordinary and the human can reveal the mystery of God and divine grace.

Like planets around the sun, our daily prayer draws us to the Sunday assembly where we gather for the word and the breaking of the bread in the changing seasons of the year. From the Sunday assembly, our daily prayer flows into the week.

> I bind unto myself today, the power of
>   God to hold and lead,
> his eye to watch, his might to stay, his
>   ear to hearken to my need;
> the wisdom of my God to teach, his
>   hand to guide, his shield to ward;
> the word of God to give me speech,
>   his heavenly host to be my guard.
>
> *Saint Patrick's Breastplate*

Daily Prayer

UPON WAKING

Upon waking, trace a small cross on the lips and say,

O Lord, open my lips,
and my mouth will declare your praise.

or

The Sacred Three be over me,
the blessing of the Trinity.

FOR EVERY DAY

O LORD, in the morning you hear my voice.
Psalm 5:3

Awake, my soul!
Awake, O harp and lyre!
I will awake the dawn.
I will give thanks to you, O Lord, among the peoples;
I will sing praises to you among the nations.
For your steadfast love is as high as the heavens:
your faithfulness extends to the clouds.
Psalm 57:8-10

The path of the righteous is like the light of dawn,
which shines brighter and brighter until the full day.
Proverbs 4:18

I bind unto myself today
the power of God to hold and lead,
his eye to watch,
his might to stay, his ear to hearken to my need.
St. Patrick's Breastplate

I give thanks to you, my heavenly Father,
through Jesus Christ your dear Son,
that you have protected me through the night
from all harm and danger

and I ask that you also protect me today from sin
    and every danger,
so that my life and actions may please you.
Into your hands I commend my body, my soul,
    and all that is mine.
Let your holy angel be with me,
so that the wicked foe may have no power over me. Amen.
Luther's morning prayer

FOR THE LORD'S DAY

O Holy Spirit, enter in
and in our hearts your work begin.
Sun of the soul, O light divine,
around and in us brightly shine.
Michael Schirmer

You alone are the Holy one,
you alone are the Lord,
you alone are the Most High.
Gloria

Send your Holy Spirit into our hearts,
that we may receive our Lord with a living faith.
Eucharistic Prayer I

Almighty God,
strengthen us in faith toward you
and in love toward one another.
Communion Prayer

Prayer in the Morning

INVITATION

Trace a small cross on the lips and say,

O Lord, I cry to you for help.
In the morning my prayer comes before you.

HYMN

This day God gives me strength of high heaven,
sun and moon shining, flame in my hearth,
flashing of lightning, wind in its swiftness,
deeps of the ocean, firmness of earth.

This day God sends me strength as my guardian,
Might to uphold me, wisdom as guide.
Your eyes are watchful, your ears are list'ning,
your lips are speaking, friend at my side.

God's way is my way, God's shield is 'round me,
God's host defends me, saving from ill.
Angels of heaven, drive from me always
all that would harm me, stand by me still.

Rising, I thank you, mighty and strong One,
king of creation, giver of rest,
firmly confessing Threeness of Persons,
Oneness of Godhead, Trinity blest.
Tune: BUNESSAN

PSALM 108:1-4

My heart is steadfast, O God, my heart is steadfast;
    I will sing and make melody.
    Awake my soul.
Awake, O harp and lyre!
    I will awake the dawn.
I will give thanks to you, O LORD, among the peoples,
    and I will sing praises to you among the nations.
For your steadfast love is higher than the heavens,
    and your faithfulness reaches to the clouds.

SCRIPTURE

Use the readings listed in Daily Readings and Prayers

THE SONG OF ZECHARIAH

> Blessed are you, Lord, the God of Israel,
> you have come to your people and set them free.
> You have raised up for us a mighty Savior,
> born of the house of your servant David.
> Through your holy prophets, you promised of old
> > to save us from our enemies,
> > from the hands of all who hate us,
> > to show mercy to our forebears,
> > and to remember your holy covenant.
> This was the oath you swore to our father Abraham:
> > to set us free from the hands of our enemies,
> > free to worship you without fear,
> > holy and righteous before you,
> > all the days of our life.
> And you, child, shall be called the prophet of the Most High,
> for you will go before the Lord to prepare the way,
> to give God's people knowledge of salvation
> by the forgiveness of their sins.
> In the tender compassion of our God
> the dawn from on high shall break upon us,
> to shine of those who dwell in darkness and the shadow of death,
> and to guide our feet into the way of peace.
> > *Benedictus, Luke 1:68-79*

PRAYERS

Prayer for others and ourselves
The Lord's Prayer

As you cause the sun to rise, O God,
bring the light of Christ to dawn in our souls
and dispel all darkness.
Give us grace to reflect Christ's glory;
and let his love show in our deeds,
his peace shine in our words,
and his healing in our touch,
that all may give him praise, now and forever. Amen
Book of Common Worship

BLESSING

May we continue to grow in the grace and knowledge
of Jesus Christ, our Lord and Savior. Amen
See *2 Peter 3:18*

At Midday

INVITATION

Whatever you do, in word or deed,
do everything in the name of the Lord Jesus.
Colossians 3:17

PSALM 23

The LORD is my shepherd, I shall not want.
    He makes me lie down in green pastures;
he leads me beside still waters;
    he restores my soul.
He leads me in right paths
    for his name's sake.

Even though I walk through the darkest valley,
    I fear no evil;
for you are with me;
    your rod and your staff—
    they comfort me.

You prepare a table before me
    in the presence of my enemies;
you anoint my head with oil;
    my cup overflows.

Surely goodness and mercy shall follow me
    all the days of my life,
and I shall dwell in the house of the LORD
    my whole life long.

SCRIPTURE

Use the readings listed in Daily Readings and Prayers

PRAYERS

Prayers for others and ourselves
The Lord's Prayer

Blessed Savior,
at this hour you hung upon the cross,
stretching out your loving arms:
Grant that all the peoples of the earth
may look to you and be saved;
for your tender mercies' sake. Amen

Heavenly Father,
in whom we live and move and have our being:
We humbly pray you so to guide and govern us by your Holy
    Spirit,
that in all the cares and occupations of our life
we may not forget you,
but remember that we are ever walking in your sight;
through Jesus Christ our Lord. Amen

BLESSING

The Lord bless us, defend us from all evil,
and bring us to everlasting life. Amen

Prayer in the Evening

INVITATION

Make the sign of the cross and say,

O God, come to my assistance.
O Lord, hasten to help me.
See *Psalm 70:1*

HYMN

Christ, mighty Savior, light of all creation,
you make the daytime radiant with the sunlight
and to the night give glittering adornment, stars in the heavens.

Now comes the day's end as the sun is setting:
mirror of daybreak, pledge of resurrection;
while in the heavens choirs of stars appearing hallow the nightfall.

Therefore we come now evening rites to offer,
joyfully chanting holy hymns to praise you,
with all creation joining hearts and voices, singing your glory.

Give heed, we pray you, to our supplication:
that you may grant us pardon for offenses,
strength for our weak hearts, rest for aching bodies,
soothing the weary.

Though bodies slumber, hearts shall keep their vigil,
forever resting in the peace of Jesus,
in light or darkness worshiping our Savior now and forever.
Tune: INNISFREE FARM

PSALM 121

I lift up my eyes to the hills—
from where will my help come?
My help comes from the LORD,
who made heaven and earth.

He will not let your foot be moved;
    he who keeps you will not slumber.
He who keeps Israel
    will neither slumber nor sleep.

The LORD is your keeper;
    the LORD is your shade at your right hand.
The sun shall not strike you by day,
    nor the moon by night.

The LORD will keep you from all evil;
    he will keep your life.
The LORD will keep your going out and your coming in
    from this time on and forevermore.

SCRIPTURE

Use the readings listed in Daily Readings and Prayers

THE SONG OF MARY

My soul proclaims the greatness of the Lord,
my spirit rejoices in God my Savior,
for you, Lord, have looked with favor on your lowly servant.
From this day all generations will call me blessed:
    you, the Almighty, have done great things for me
    and holy is your name.
    You have mercy on those who fear you,
    from generation to generation.
You have shown the strength of your arm
and scattered the proud in their conceit,
casting down the mighty from their thrones
and lifting up the lowly.
You have filled the hungry with good things
and sent the rich away empty.
You have come to the aid of your servant Israel,
to remember the promise of mercy,
the promise made to our forebears,
to Abraham and his children for ever.
      Magnificat, Luke 1:46-55

PRAYERS

Prayers for others and ourselves
The Lord's Prayer

Keep watch, dear Lord,
with those who work, or watch, or weep this night,
and give your angels charge over those who sleep.
Tend the sick, Lord Christ;
give rest to the weary, bless the dying,
soothe the suffering, pity the afflicted,
shield the joyous;
and all for your love's sake. Amen

Book of Common Prayer

O God, the life of all who live,
the light of the faithful, the strength of those who labor,
and the repose of the dead:
We thank you for the blessings of the day that is past,
and humbly ask for your protection through the coming night.
Bring us in safety to the morning hours;
through him who died and rose again for us,
your Son our Savior Jesus Christ. Amen

Book of Common Prayer

BLESSING

May the peace of God,
which surpasses all understanding,
guard our hearts and minds in Christ Jesus.

See *Philippians 4:7*

At Bedtime

INVITATION

When going to bed, make the sign of the cross and say,

The Lord almighty grant us a quiet night
and peace at the last.

PSALM 91:1-6, 9-12

You who live in the shelter of the Most High,
  who abide in the shadow of the Almighty,
will say to the LORD, "My refuge and my fortress;
  my God, in whom I trust."
For he will deliver you from the snare of the fowler
  and from the deadly pestilence;
he will cover with his pinions,
  and under his wings you will find refuge;
  his faithfulness is a shield and buckler.
You will not fear the terror of the night,
  or the arrow that flies by day,
or the pestilence that stalks in darkness,
  or the destruction that wastes at noonday.

Because you have made the LORD your refuge,
  the Most High your dwelling place,
no evil shall befall you,
  no scourge come near your tent.

For he will command his angels concerning you
  to guard you in all your ways.
On their hands they will bear you up,
  so that you will not dash your foot against a stone.

SCRIPTURE

*Use the readings listed in Daily Readings and Prayer or Matthew 11:28-30;
Romans 8:38-39; Hebrews 13:20-21; 1 Peter 5:6-9a*

RESPONSE

Into your hands, O Lord, I commend my spirit.
You have redeemed me, O Lord, God of truth.
Into your hands I commend my spirit.

THE SONG OF SIMEON

Guide us waking, O Lord,
and guard us sleeping;
that awake we may watch with Christ
and asleep we may rest in peace.

Now, Lord, you let your servant go in peace;
your word has been fulfilled.
My own eyes have seen the salvation
which you have prepared in the sight of every people:
a light to reveal you to the nations
and the glory of your people Israel.
Nunc dimittis, Luke 2:29-32

PRAYERS

Prayers for others and ourselves
The Lord's Prayer

Visit this house,
we beg you, Lord,
and banish from it
the deadly power of the evil one.
May your holy angels dwell here
to keep us in peace,
and may your blessing be always upon us.
We ask this through Christ our Lord. Amen

I give thanks to you, my heavenly Father,
through Jesus Christ your dear Son,
that you have graciously protected me today,
and I ask you to forgive me all my sins, where I have done wrong,
and graciously to protect me tonight.
For into your hands I commend myself:
my body, my soul, and all that is mine.
Let your holy angel be with me,
so that the wicked foe may have no power over me. Amen
Luther's evening prayer

BLESSING

The almighty and merciful Lord, Father, Son, and Holy Spirit,
bless us and keep us. Amen

Bedtime Prayer with Children

SONGS

All praise to you, my God, this night
for all the blessings of the light.
Keep me, oh, keep me, King of kings,
beneath your own almighty wings.
       Tune: TALLIS' CANON

God, who made the earth and heaven, darkness and light:
You the day for work have given, for rest the night.
May your angel guards defend us, slumber sweet
    your mercy send us,
holy dreams and hopes attend us, all through the night.
       Tune: AR HYD Y NOS

This little light of mine, I'm gonna let it shine,
this little light of mine, I'm gonna let it shine,
this little light of mine, I'm gonna let it shine,
let it shine, let shine, let it shine.
       Tune: African American spiritual

Children of the heav'nly Father
safely in his bosom gather;
nestling bird nor star in heaven
such a refuge ne'er was given.
       Tune: TRYGGARE KAN INGEN VARA

Sun of my soul, O Savior dear,
it is not night if you are near;
O may no earthborn cloud arise,
to hide you from your servant's eyes.
       Tune: TALLIS' CANON

Thy holy wings, O Savior, spread gently over me
and let me rest securely through good and ill in thee.
Oh, be my strength and portion, my rock and hiding place,
and let my ev'ry moment be lived within thy grace.

Oh, wash me in the waters of Noah's cleansing flood.
Give me a willing spirit, a heart both clean and good.
Oh, take into thy keeping thy children great and small,
and while we sweetly slumber, enfold us one and all.
Tune: BRED DINA VIDA VINGAR or AURELIA

PRAYERS

Keep me as the apple of your eye.
Hide me, O LORD, in the shadow of your wings.
See *Psalm 17:8*

The LORD is my shepherd, I need nothing more.
Psalm 23:1

The LORD is my light and my salvation;
whom shall I fear?
Psalm 27:1

Stay with us, Lord.
Luke 24:29

Lord, you know that I love you.
John 21:16

Come, Lord Jesus, and night shall be no more.
See *Revelation 21:5*

Be near me, Lord Jesus: I ask you to stay
close by me forever and love me, I pray.
Bless all the dear children in your tender care
and fit us for heaven to live with you there.

Angel sent by God to guide me,
be my light and walk beside me;
be my guardian and protect me;
on the paths of life direct me.

Jesus Christ, a child so wise,
bless my hands and fill my eyes.
Watch me as I sleep in bed,
help me in the days ahead.

BLESSINGS

As you trace a cross on the child's forehead, say one of these blessings

Receive the cross of Christ.

The LORD bless you and keep you,
now and forever.
> See *Numbers 6:24*

May the God of peace give you very good thing.
> *Hebrews 13:20*

God is love,
and those who abide in love abide in God,
and God abides in them.
> *1 John 4:16*

Let your light shine before others.
> *Matthew 5:16*

The grace of the Lord Jesus Christ,
the love of God,
and the communion of the Holy Spirit be with you.
> *2 Corinthians 13:13*

May the Lord of peace
give you peace at all times in all ways.
> *2 Thessalonians 3:16*

Peace be with you.
> *John 20:21*

Sunday

*F*rom the earliest days of our history, Christians have called Sunday "the Lord's Day," the first day of the week when God created light. Ancient Christians called the day of Christ's resurrection "the eighth day," a new day in which God brought life and light out of death and darkness. As scripture attests, Christ appears on the first day of the week—Sunday—to his followers. He gathers them through the power of the Spirit, he explains the scriptures and breaks bread, he offers his gift of peace, and sends his disciples forth into the world to continue his mission. Sunday remains for Christians the day on which we celebrate our immersion in his life through baptism and our sustenance in that life through the supper. Sunday marks the public gathering of Christians and the renewal of their mission in the rhythm of daily life.

Christians celebrate the Lord's Day from the setting of the sun on Saturday evening until nightfall on Sunday. We mark this day from sunset to sunset in various ways: with prayer, song, reading from the scriptures, renewing our baptism, and joining other Christians for worship. We may celebrate the day of resurrection with a simple invocation of Christ's name or a festive meal surrounded with lights, prayers, and songs. While we gather with the baptized on the Lord's Day for the celebration of word and meal, we also recognize that the risen Christ appears in the many ordinary places of life: in houses and apartments, in a garden and by a lake, in the sharing of a meal, walking with friends on a road

(Luke 24; John 20-21). Celebrating Sunday in the home brings to greater awareness the presence of Christ among us and with us in our daily tasks and gatherings.

The celebration of Sunday may begin with the lighting of a candle and a prayer to Christ the Light at the Saturday evening meal or at bedtime. On festive occasions, one may use more lights, a bowl of water, and a greater selection of songs, psalms, and readings. On Sunday morning, one may offer a brief prayer or read a psalm. As the day comes to a close, one may light a candle and pray or sing to Christ the Light, read a selection from the Bible, or repeat a short verse of scripture.

Sunday Morning

INVITATION

Make the sign of the cross and say,

This is the day the LORD has made;
let us rejoice and be glad.
Psalm 118:24

HYMN

Come, let us join our cheerful songs
with angels round the throne;
ten thousand thousand are their tongues,
but all their joys are one.

"Worthy the Lamb that died," they cry,
"to be exalted thus!"
"Worthy the Lamb," our lips reply,
"for he was slain for us!"

Let all creation join in one
to bless the sacred name
of him who sits upon the throne,
and to adore the Lamb.
Tune: NUN DANKET ALL

PSALM 63:1-5

O God, you are my God, I seek you,
my soul thirsts for you;
my flesh faints for you,
as in a dry and weary land where there is no water.
So I have looked upon you in the sanctuary,
beholding your power and glory.

Because your steadfast love is better than life,
my lips will praise you.
So I will bless you as long as I live;
I will lift up my hands and call on your name.

My soul is satisfied as with a rich feast,
and my mouth praises you with joyful lips.

SCRIPTURE

Use the readings listed in Daily Readings and Prayers

CANTICLE

The Song of Zechariah (page 21) or

This is the feast of victory for our God.
Alleluia, alleluia, alleluia.

Worthy is Christ, the Lamb who was slain,
whose blood set us free to be people of God.
Refrain

Power, riches, wisdom, and strength,
and honor, blessing, and glory are his.
Refrain

Sing with all the people of God,
and join in the hymn of all creation.
Blessing, honor, glory, and might
be to God and the Lamb forever. Amen
Refrain

For the Lamb who was slain has begun his reign.
Alleluia.
Refrain

PRAYERS

Prayers for others and ourselves
The Lord's Prayer

In the beginning, O God,
you created light on this day.
Your mighty hand raised Christ from the grave
on the first day of the week
and filled all creation with the light of life.
Come to us, we pray, and lead us to that day
when all creation will rejoice in the feast of victory. Amen

BLESSING

May God who has given us a new birth into a living hope
through the death and resurrection of Jesus Christ,
bless us and keep us now and forever. Amen
See *1 Peter 1:3*

THANKSGIVING FOR BAPTISM

Gather around a bowl of water and a lighted candle

O give thanks to the Lord, for he is good,
for his mercy endures forever.
Psalm 136:1

Blessed are you, O Lord our God,
creator of all things,
for on this day you brought forth a new creation in Christ.
Through baptism you have made us your children,
dead to sin and alive to you.
You have washed us,
filled us with your love,
and sustained us with your Spirit.
Therefore we praise you
and give you our loving thanks,
for your mercy endures forever. Amen

Each person may dip a hand into the water and make the sign of the cross in remembrance of baptism.

SUNDAY TABLE PRAYER

Lord, we give you thanks, for you are good,
your steadfast love endures forever.
It is you who remembered us in our low estate,
for your steadfast love endures forever;
and rescued us from our foes,
for your steadfast love endures forever;
who gives food to all living things,
for your steadfast love endures forever.
We give thanks to you the God of heaven,
for your steadfast love endures forever. Amen
See *Psalm 136:1, 23-26*

Sunday Evening

INVITATION

At the setting of the sun light a candle and say,

Jesus Christ is the light of the world,
the light no darkness can overcome.

THANKSGIVING FOR LIGHT

We give you thanks, God of heaven and earth,
for on this the first day of creation you created light
and separated day from night;
you brought forth Jesus Christ from the tomb,
the true Sun that enlightens the world;
you inspired the apostles
with the bright fire of the Holy Spirit.
Fill us now with your light that all may see our good works
and give glory to you, through Jesus Christ our Lord. Amen

HYMN

O Trinity, O blessed Light,
O Unity of princely might:
the fiery sun is going down;
shed light upon us through your Son.

To you our morning song of praise,
to you our evening prayer we raise;
we praise your light in every age,
the glory of our pilgrimage.

All glory be to God above
and to the Son, the prince of love,
and to the Spirit One in Three!
We praise you, blessed Trinity.

Tune: O HEILIGE DREIFALTIGKEIT

PSALM 112:1-7

Happy are those who fear the LORD,
> who greatly delight in his commandments.

Their descendants will be mighty in the land;
> the generation of the upright will be blessed.
Wealth and riches are in their houses,
> and their righteousness endures forever.

They rise in the darkness as light for the upright;
> they are gracious, merciful, and righteous.
It is well with those who deal generously and lend,
> who conduct their affairs with justice.

For the righteous will never be moved;
> they will be remembered forever.
They are not afraid of evil tidings;
> their hearts are firm, secure in the LORD.

SCRIPTURE

Use the readings listed in Daily Readings and Prayers

CANTICLE

The Song of Mary (page 26) or

Give thanks to the Father,
who has enabled you to share
in the inheritance of the saints in light.
He has rescued us from the power of darkness
and transferred us into the kingdom of his beloved Son,
in whom we have redemption, the forgiveness of our sins.

He is the image of the invisible God,
the firstborn of all creation;
for in him all things were created,
things visible and invisible,
whether thrones or dominions or rulers or powers;
all things have been created through him and for him.

He himself is before all things,
and in him all things hold together.
He is the head of the body, the church;
he is the beginning, the firstborn from the dead,
so that he might come to have first place in everything.

For in him all the fullness of God was pleased to dwell,
and through him God was pleased to reconcile to himself
all things, whether on earth or in heaven,
by making peace through the blood of his cross.
Colossians 1:12-20

PRAYERS

Prayers for others and ourselves
The Lord's Prayer

Lord God,
whose Son our Savior Jesus Christ triumphed
    over the powers of death
and prepared for us our place in the new Jerusalem:
Grant that we, who have this day given thanks for the resurrection,
may praise you in that City of which he is the light,
where he lives and reigns with you and the Holy Spirit,
one God now and for ever. Amen

BLESSING

May the Lord of peace
give us peace at all times in all ways.
See *2 Thessalonians 3:16*

The Prayers of Christians

KYRIE

Lord, have mercy.
Christ, have mercy.
Lord, have mercy.

GLORIA PATRI

Glory to the Father, and to the Son,
and to the Holy Spirit;
as it was in the beginning, is now,
and will be forever. Amen

APOSTLES' CREED

I believe in God, the Father almighty,
    creator of heaven and earth.

I believe in Jesus Christ, God's only Son, our Lord,
    who was conceived by the Holy Spirit,
    born of the Virgin Mary,
    suffered under Pontius Pilate,
    was crucified, died, and was buried;
    he descended to the dead.
    On the third day he rose again;
    he ascended into heaven,
    he is seated at the right hand of the Father,
    and he will come to judge the living and the dead.

I believe in the Holy Spirit,
    the holy catholic Church,
    the communion of saints,
    the forgiveness of sins,
    the resurrection of the body,
    and the life everlasting. Amen.

SANCTUS

Holy, holy, holy Lord, God of power and might,
heaven and earth are full of your glory.
Hosanna in the highest.

Blessed is he who comes in the name of the Lord.
Hosanna in the highest.

THE LORD'S PRAYER

Our Father in heaven,
hallowed be your name,
your kingdom come,
your will be done,
on earth as in heaven.
Give us today our daily bread.
Forgive us our sins
as we forgive those who sin against us.
Save us from the time of trial
and deliver us from evil.
For the kingdom, the power, and the glory are yours,
now and for ever. Amen

LAMB OF GOD

Lamb of God, you take away the sin of the world,
have mercy on us.
Lamb of God, you take away the sin of the world,
have mercy on us.
Lamb of God, you take away the sin of the world,
grant us peace.

Advent

*There are three parts
to this season—
the waiting,
and the waiting,
and the waiting.*

*T*he cycle of seasons called the church year is shaped by the life of Jesus Christ. It has grown over thousands of years out of a convergence of the Christ story with the natural seasons of the northern hemisphere, the festivals of pre-Christian religions, and the holy days of the Jewish calendar. Its festivals force us to confront life's deepest questions and truths. If we let them, they will give shape and rhythm to our lives, which can often seem scattered and chaotic. And in the rich imagery of their stories, the festivals and seasons offer us limitless possibility to face and reexamine the truths and realities of existence.

It is as when white light passes through a prism, and different colors are refracted out, separated, and made visible. When the light of the biblical stories told during the year passes through the shape of our present lives, different truths are refracted out, separated, and made visible. We never enter the church's year of grace as exactly the same person we were twelve months before. The depth and richness of these seasons and feast days have something to say to us at each stage of life, from infant to elder. We never exhaust the potential of these stories to shape and transform us.

As we cross the threshold into Advent and encounter the readings from Luke and the prophets, we ask in all innocence, what do they say to us this year? Where are we in these stories? How are these stories with us today? Since Advent means "coming," what is the coming we await? So, in this year, in this person's life, in this culture, this reflection on Advent and its coming is but one reflection among many.

The human experience of longing is at the center of Advent's days. For a child, it may be longing for the coming birth of Jesus, and that is enough. But as the child grows, other questions emerge, and the longing deepens and broadens. As we age, we discover that possessions do not satisfy our hunger; we long for something more. We may long for justice and righteousness as did Malachi and Jeremiah; we may long for a future that is more than the sum of past and present. We may long for the completion of all things. And, yes, we may long for peace.

This longing in Advent is perhaps the church at odds with North American culture. In a time that says "now," Advent says "wait." To an age that says "consume," Advent says "hope for something you may never see yourself." To an era that says "conform," Advent says "Blessed is she who believed that there would be a fulfillment of what was spoken to her by the Lord" (Luke 1:45).

Blue as the color for Advent gives us direction for our longing, for blue is the color both of the depths of the sea and the heights of the sky. Our yearning reaches to the profound and to the lofty, to the very origin and to the airy heaven. It is a longing for what we were intended to be, for what we could become, and for what is making its way into the present. Blue is the color of innocence and of devotion, and thus usually clothes Mary, the Mother of our Lord. Our yearning encompasses the desire to be, like her, so entirely at the service of God that holiness might enter the world through us.

The longing of this season is often portrayed in scripture and poetry as a longing for light. This is natural in the brief, sometimes dim, winter daylight in the Northern hemisphere. Nothing can grow green without the sun, and we await its return. So the Romans celebrated at the end of these days the Feast of the Unconquered Sun, and the Celts, the winter solstice bonfires. The Jewish people light the menorah during this time to celebrate the continuing light of their religion, almost snuffed out by a Roman emperor. Christians light the four Advent candles, increasing in radiance over the dark weeks, until the merciful light that is the life of all returns.

To long for light is to long for illumination, for our true faces to be made visible. To long for light is to long for fulfillment, for wholeness. To long for light is to long for transformation, to be refined in the refiner's fire and to present offerings to the Lord in righteousness.

Over the centuries, Christians have celebrated three Advents: the past coming of the Christ, born in Bethlehem; the present coming of Christ in the sacramental meal; and the future coming of Christ, at the completion of all things. As children, we long for the baby Jesus and for our own delight. When we grow to adults, we long for the present and for the good of self and community. When we become wise, we will long for the light that illumines all creation, a good

and gracious gift that our eyes may not see now. And this is
the name by which it shall be called: The Lord is our righteousness.

There are three parts
to this season—
the yearning,
and the yearning,
and the yearning.

Praying in Advent

INVITATION

In the tender compassion of our God,
the dawn from on high shall break upon us.
Luke 1:78

TABLE PRAYER

O God our hope,
we look for signs of your coming among us.
May this food and drink refresh us and fill us with gratitude,
as we eagerly wait and watch for the promised day of salvation
in Jesus Christ our Lord. Amen

HYMN

People, look east. The time is near
of the crowning of the year.
Make your house fair as you are able,
trim the hearth and set the table.
People, look east, and sing today—
Love, the Guest, is on the way.

Furrows be glad. Though earth is bare,
one more seed is planted there.
Give up your strength the seed to nourish,
that in course the flower may flourish.
People, look east, and sing today-
Love, the Rose, is on the way.

Stars, keep watch. When night is dim,
one more light the bowl shall brim,
singing beyond the frosty weather,
bright as sun and moon together.
People, look east, and sing today-
Love, the Star, is on the way.

Angels announce with shouts of mirth
him who brings new life to earth.
Set ev'ry peak and valley humming
with the word, the Lord is coming.
People, look east, and sing today—
Love, the Lord, is on the way.
Tune: Besançon

PSALM 80:1-3

Give ear, O Shepherd of Israel,
    you who lead Joseph like a flock!
You who are enthroned upon the cherubim, shine forth
    before Ephraim and Benjamin and Manasseh.
Stir up your might,
    and come and save us!

Restore us, O God;
    let your face shine, that we may be saved.

SCRIPTURE

See the daily readings

CANTICLE

In the morning, the Song of Zechariah (page 21)
In the evening, the Song of Mary (page 26)
At bedtime, the Song of Simeon (page 29) or

Hear the word of the Lord, O nations,
    and declare it in the coastlands far away;
say, "He who scattered Israel with gather him,
    and will keep him as a shepherd a flock."
For the Lord has ransomed Jacob,
    and has redeemed him from hands too strong for him.

They shall come and sing aloud on the height of Zion,
    and they shall be radiant over the goodness of the Lord,
over the grain, the wine, and the oil,
    and over the young of the flock and the herd;
their life shall become like a watered garden,
    and they shall never languish again.

Then shall the young women rejoice in the dance,
and the young men and the old shall be merry.
I will turn their mourning into joy,
I will comfort them, and give them gladness for sorrow.
I will give the priests their fill of fatness,
and my people shall be satisfied with my bounty,
says the Lord.

Jeremiah 31:10-14

PRAYER

Prayers for others and ourselves
The Lord's Prayer

O God most high,
for you we wait, for your coming we watch,
for your reign we prepare, in your promise we rejoice.
Open our eyes that we may see you.
Open our hearts that we may receive you.
Open our lips that we may praise you.
Open our hands that we may serve you. Amen

BLESSING OF THE ADVENT WREATH

This prayer may be said each week as a new candle on the Advent wreath is lighted

O faithful and loving God,
we praise you for your tender compassion
and give you thanks for your steadfast love for us and all creation.
Bless us who see the light of this wreath,
that we may be strengthened by the hope of your advent
among us,
and live toward the completion of all things in you.
We ask this through Christ our Lord. Amen

BLESSING OF THE JESSE TREE

During Advent an evergreen tree may be decorated with images from the O-antiphons and the Hebrew scripture readings of Advent. On Christmas Eve, these images are replaced by Christmas ornaments. Place one or more symbols on the tree and say,

Blessed are you, LORD our God, creator of the universe,
from the beginning you have sustained creation
    through your Word.
You spoke, and all was created.
You called, and from Abraham and Sarah arose a great nation.
You led, and your people Israel were brought to freedom.
You promised, and from Israel came the Christ.
Bless now your people who long for your day of justice and peace.
May your promises of old encourage us to a living hope
and confident joy, through Christ our Lord. Amen

THE O-ANTIPHONS

During the final week of Advent, an O-antiphon is sung each day, usually in the evening before the song of Mary

December 17

O Wisdom, pow'r of God Most High,
embracing all things far and nigh;
in strength and beauty come and stay;
teach us your will and guide our ways.
Rejoice! Rejoice! Emmanuel shall come to you, O Israel!

December 18

O Lord of Israel, come in might
as to your tribes on Sinai's height,
in ancient times you gave the law,
in cloud, and majesty, and awe.
Refrain

December 19

O Flower of Jesse, come and free,
your own from Satan's tyranny.
We trust your mighty power to save
and give us vict'ry o'er the grave.
Refrain

December 20

O Key of David, Holy One,
come, open wide our heavenly home;
make safe the way that leads on high,
and close the path to misery.
Refrain

December 21
O Daypsring, come with light and cheer;
O Sun of Justice, now draw near.
Disperse the gloomy clouds of night,
and death's dark shadow put to flight.
Refrain

December 22
O Ruler of the nations, come;
O Cornerstone that binds in one:
refresh the hearts that long for you;
restore the broken, make us new.
Refrain

December 23
O come, O come, Emmanuel,
and ransom captive Israel
that mourns in lonely exile here
until the Son of God appear.
Refrain

Daily Readings and Prayers

First Sunday of Advent

S	Jer. 33:14-16		Ps. 25:1-10
	I Thess. 3:9-13		Luke 21:25-36
M	Num. 17:1-11	**T**	2 Sam. 7:18-29
W	Luke 29:32	**Th**	Isa. 1:24-31
F	2 Peter 3:14-18	**S**	Ps. 25

FOR PRAYER THROUGHOUT THE DAY

Show me your ways, O Lord, and teach me your wisdom.
See *Psalm 25:3*

A PRAYER FOR THE WEEK

God of love,
strengthen our hearts in holiness.
Prepare us to meet the Lord Jesus when he comes again with all his
saints. Amen

Second Sunday of Advent

S	Mal. 3:1-4		Luke 1:68-79
	Phil. 1:3-11		Luke 3:1-6
M	Isa. 40:1-11	**T**	Isa. 19:18-24
W	Luke 7:18-30	**Th**	Num. 3:5-13
F	2 Peter 4:1-11	**S**	Ps. 126

FOR PRAYER THROUGHOUT THE DAY

The dawn from on high shall break upon us.
Luke 1:78

A PRAYER FOR THE WEEK

God who comes to us from the future,
make your church a holy and merciful temple,
a people eager to prepare your way. Amen

Third Sunday of Advent

S	Zeph. 3:14-20		Isa. 12:2-6
	Phil. 4:4-7		Luke 3:7-18
M	Num. 16:1-14	**T**	Num 16:20-35
W	Luke 7:31-35	**Th**	Micah 4:10-13
F	I Peter 4:1-11	**S**	Ps. 85

FOR PRAYER THROUGHOUT THE DAY

Bring us home, O God.
> See *Zephaniah 3:14, 20*

A PRAYER FOR THE WEEK

God in whom we rejoice,
your peace surpasses our understanding.
Prepare the hearts of your people to announce with joy
that you are always near. Amen

Fourth Sunday of Advent

S	Micah 5:2-5a		Luke 1:47-55
	Heb. 10:5-10		Luke 1:39-45 [46-55]
M	Gen. 25.19-28	**T**	Gen. 30:1-24
W	Luke 1:5-25	**Th**	Isa. 42:14-16
F	Rom. 8:18-27	**S**	Ps. 113

FOR PRAYER THROUGHOUT THE DAY

My spirit magnifies the Lord.
> *Luke 1:46*

A PRAYER FOR THE WEEK

Come to us, faithful and loving God.
Fill us with the treasure of Christ's life
and bless us with faith, hope, and love. Amen

Christmas

*C*hristmas is the beginning of the fulfillment of all our longing. It is the celebration of our continuing relationship with God and the world. Christmas night flashes the white and silver of glory and splits the midnight blue of our awaiting. "Glory!" sing the angels. "Glory!" sing the shepherds. "Glory!" sings the psalmist. "Glory!" sings Simeon. "Glory!" we sing, as we share the bread and cup. "Glory" is nothing less than God becoming one with us in our humanity, offering us the gifts of body and blood.

Glory can also terrify; glory can blind. The shepherds trembled. "No one has ever seen God. It is God the only Son, who is close to the Father's heart, who has made him known" (John 1:18). And we have seen his glory. It is like looking at the stars at night. If one tries to look directly at a star, it twinkles, fades, and disappears, because the light overwhelms the capacity of the eye to behold directly. But if one gazes slightly to the side of the star, indirectly, it becomes clear and steady, visible and light. The range of visible light is but a tiny portion of the entire spectrum, present in a form the human eye can see. Light dawned for the righteous that night, in a form the human heart can see.

The glory of the Christmas coming, with angels bright and songful, does not cease with the fading of the angels' song. The shepherds left, we are told, "glorifying and praising God for all that they had heard and seen." We, like the shepherds, should be moved by the Nativity to such a response. Paul reminds us in Ephesians that our response is to be exactly that of the shepherds: "In Christ we have also gained an inheritance . . . so that we might live for the praise of his glory." Praise seems an unusual purpose to live for. Yet it is stated clearly: we are to live, like the radiant shepherds, for the praise of Christ's glory.

How can a person do this? Our technological age, filled with dazzling creations and numerous toys, often numbs us to the glory round about us. The festival of Christmas dazzles us awake, and for twelve days of divine light we are given the opportunity to practice seeing God's glory and praising it. For twelve complete days we rediscover and revel in a sense of wonder.

Wonder, the surprised awe of human response to God, is at the root of praise. Wonder is at the heart of Christmas; not for one day only, but for each awaking day.

What is the glory of God? At the heart of Christ's birth is the truth that God makes extraordinary things happen in ordinary places. God's "glory" is God coming to us with love through ordinary words and actions. Indeed, the wonder of Christmas desires to creep into every living moment, so that we behold the glory of God, and praise. The wonder of this holy day points to the wonder in all days; the wonder of the Bethlehem stable teaches us to find the wonder in all places; the wonder of Mary, Joseph, and Jesus leads to the wonder in the faces of ordinary people.

Christmas is not so much about the birth of Jesus two thousand years ago, as it is about the startling activity of God that continues in every place today. Christmas refocuses our vision so that we again feel wonder and see the glory of God in the daily miracles of life. Praise for glory. Praise for Christ.

Praise for life. Praise for God who is not a god far-off, watching us from a distance, but rather among us, among us, among us. The extraordinary in the ordinary. Heaven and earth in little space. The manger as its sign. "Glory!" we sing.

There is no rose of such virtue
As is the rose that bare Jesu.
Alleluia.
For in this rose contained was
Heaven and earth in little space.
Res miranda. O wondrous thing.

Praying in Christmas

INVITATION

The people who walked in darkness have seen a great light,
those who lived in a land of deep darkness—
    on them has light shined.
        Isaiah 9:2

TABLE PRAYER

O God of wonder,
the birth of your Son fills the world with joy.
With thanks and praise we bless you
for Christ's presence among us at this table.
May our Christmas feast nourish us,
that sharing your gifts,
all creation may sing the angels' song of peace and goodwill. Amen

HYMN

Angels we have heard on high, singing sweetly through the night,
and the mountains in reply, echoing their brave delight.
Gloria in excelsis Deo; Gloria in excelsis Deo.

Shepherds, why this jubilee? Why these songs of happy cheer?
What great brightness did you see? What glad tidings did you hear?
Refrain

Come to Bethlehem and see him whose birth the angels sing;
come, adore on bended knee Christ, the Lord, the newborn king.
Refrain

PSALM 97:1, 6-12

The Lord is king! Let the earth rejoice;
    let the coastlands be glad!

The heavens proclaim his righteousness;
    and the peoples behold his glory.
All worshipers of images are put to shame,
    those who make their boast in worthless idols;
    all gods bow down before him.

Zion hears and is glad,
    and the towns of Judah rejoice,
    because of your judgments, O God.
For you, O LORD, are most high over all the earth;
    you are exalted far above all gods.

The LORD loves those who hate evil;
    he guards the lives of the faithful;
    he rescues them from the hand of the wicked.
Light dawns for the righteous,
    and joy for the upright in heart.
Rejoice in the LORD, O you righteous,
    and give thanks to his holy name!

SCRIPTURE

See the daily readings

CANTICLE

    In the morning, the Song of Zechariah (page 21)
    In the evening, the Song of Mary (page 26)
    At bedtime, the Song of Simeon (page 29) or

Blessed be the God and Father of our Lord Jesus Christ,
who has blessed us in Christ
with every spiritual blessing in the heavenly places,
just as he chose us in Christ before the foundation of the world
to be holy and blameless before him in love.

He destined us for adoption as children through Jesus Christ,
according to the good pleasure of his will,
to the praise of his glorious grace
that he freely betowed on us in the Beloved.

In him we have redemption through his blood,
the forgiveness of our trespasses
according to the riches of his grace that he lavished upon us.

With all wisdom and insight
he has made known to us the mystery of his will,
according to his good pleasure that he set forth in Christ,
as a plan for the fullness of time,
to gather up all things in him,
things in heaven and things on earth.
Ephesians 1:3-10

PRAYER

Prayers for others and ourselves
The Lord's Prayer

Most Holy God,
praise to you for the glory of this holy birth;
praise to you for the miracle of God-with-us.
As the shepherds departed the stable in wonder and in joy,
so may we live our lives in praise of your glory,
for you are God with us,
eternal yet present,
almighty yet tender. Amen

BLESSING OF THE CHRISTMAS TREE

Use this reading and blessing when you first light the tree and whenever you
gather at the tree for Christmas prayer

Let the heavens be glad, and let the earth rejoice;
let the sea roar, and all that fills it;
let the field exult, and everything in it.
Then shall all the trees of the forest sing for joy
before the LORD, for he is coming,
for he is coming to judge the earth.
He will judge the world with righteousness,
and the peoples with his truth.
Psalm 96:11-13

Be praised, O God, for the blessings around us that point to you.
Be praised, O God, for the signs of this holy season that awaken in
    us wonder.
Praise for the steadfast green of this tree,
like your love, enduring all seasons.
Praise for the light that illumines our darkness,

like Christ, who brings light to the world.
Join our voices with those of the trees and all of creation,
who sing at your coming:
Glory to God in the highest, and peace to God's people on earth.
Amen

BLESSING OF THE GIFTS

Use this blessing before you open gifts.

O God, the Giver of all good gifts,
as you have so richly blessed us with signs of your love,
so may these gifts carry with them a message of abundant love
and care,
for the sake of Jesus Christ, whose wondrous birth we celebrate.
Amen

BLESSING OF THE NATIVITY SCENE

*Use this blessing when figures are added to the nativity scene throughout the
days of Christmas and on the day of Epiphany*

Bless us, O God, bless us who gather around this stable.
As we celebrate Christ's birth into the world,
may we receive the Christ Child into our hearts with gratitude and
song. Amen

BLESSING FOR THE NEW YEAR

Use this blessing on New Year's Eve or New Year's Day

Into your hands, O God, we commend the coming year.
May we see each day as a blessing and a gift.
May we remember in all we do the holiness of life.
O most merciful God, into your hands we commend our days.
May they be filled with an awareness of your presence
and an eagerness to serve you well. Amen

Daily Readings and Prayers

Christmas Day

Dec. 25	Isa. 52:7-10		Ps. 98
	Heb. 1:1-4		John 1:1-14
Dec. 26	Luke 2:1-20	**Dec. 27**	Luke 3:23-38
Dec. 28	Ps. 96	**Dec. 29**	Gen. 1:1-2:4a
Dec. 30	Ps. 97	**Dec. 31**	Heb. 1:1-12

FOR PRAYER THROUGHOUT THE DAY

> Glory to God in the highest heaven.
> *Luke 2:14*

A PRAYER FOR THE WEEK

> Emmanuel, God with us,
> you are great joy for all people.
> Transform us with your grace
> so that we may be your good news of great joy for the world. Amen

The Name of Jesus

Jan. 1   Num. 6:22-27
　　　　　Ps. 8
　　　　　Gal. 4:4-7
　　　　　Luke 2:15-21

First Sunday after Christmas

S	I Sam. 2:18-20, 26		Ps. 148
	Col. 3:12-17		Luke 2:41-52
M	I Chron. 28:1-10	**T**	2 Chron. 7:1-11
W	Luke 8:19-21	**Th**	Ezek. 43:1-12
F	Heb. 9:1-14	**S**	Ps. 11

FOR PRAYER THROUGHOUT THE DAY

Clothe us with the compassion of Christ.
See *Colossians 3:12*

A PRAYER FOR THE WEEK

God our Father,
you bless the world in Christ, the newborn Son.
Plant the seed of your word in our hearts
that we may grow in grace and wisdom. Amen

Second Sunday after Christmas

S	Jer. 31:7-14	Ps. 147:13-21
	Eph. 1:3-14	John 1:[1-9] 10-18

FOR PRAYER THROUGHOUT THE DAY

Christ with us, may we see your glory.
See *John 1:14*

A PRAYER FOR THE WEEK

O God,
your Word reveals your love for all people.
Open our hearts to receive this love
that our lives may reveal the glory of your only Son. Amen

Epiphany

Arise, shine; for your light has come, and the glory of the Lord has risen upon you. For darkness shall cover the earth, and thick darkness the peoples; but the Lord will arise upon you, and his glory will appear over you.
Isaiah 60:1-2

*I*n the dark, the human eye can perceive the light of a candle ten miles away. So attuned is the human eye to light, we see the light and are immediately drawn to it. And what is the effect of even so tiny a pinpoint of light upon us? Our attention is immediately drawn outside of ourselves. Arise, shine, your light has come, proclaims Isaiah. As the light brightens, we begin to perceive its source, and we become aware of our surroundings. Things and people receive names, because the light shows us their identity. Our awareness alters. And the light identifies us as well.

From the outset, the stories we hear during the Epiphany season draw us again and again to the revealing of an identity. Who is this person born in Bethlehem, "a light to reveal [God] to the nations"? The magi bring gifts of identity: gold for a king, frankincense for a priest, myrrh for the embalming of an ordinary mortal body. As the light poured from the opened heavens above Jesus' baptism, a voice said, "You are my Son, my Beloved." At the wedding in Cana, John records that Jesus did the first of his signs, the changing of water into fine wine. On through the stories of Jesus' reading from the Isaiah scroll to the wondrous catch of fish on Galilee, to his radiant appearance on the mountain with Moses and Elijah—Jesus' identity is revealed.

Epiphany means "revelation" or "appearing." But the "appearing" of Jesus is not simply a revelation of his identity as the light of the world. Light shines on its surroundings, giving them a reflected glow, which in turn brings light to other surroundings. "All of us, with unveiled faces, seeing the glory of the Lord as though reflected in a mirror, are being transformed into the same image from one degree of glory to another" (2 Corinthians 3:18). Epiphany is also about our identity as children of the light. The glory of the Lord causes us also to shine with light. We are called today no differently than the disciples were called two thousand years ago. Not only were the disciples transformed, but we also are transformed by the coming of the light. Arise, shine, we are told.

When we live as people upon whom the light has shined, we see differently. We become aware. Like Isaiah, we become aware that the whole earth is full of God's glory; like the psalmist we become aware of the weak and the needy who are precious in God's sight; like Jesus, we become aware of the poor, the hungry, the mourning, the hated who are blessed in God's sight; like Paul, we become aware that the glory of God reflects from us as love. The light shines, and draws our attention outside of ourselves. The light shines, and we become aware of the faces around us. The light shines, and we are called to live as images of that light, radiating love.

Just as the magi brought gifts to Jesus for the living out of his life, so too are we given gifts for the living out of our lives as children of the Most High. Diverse gifts. Gifts of the Spirit. Gifts to be used for the common good. *Common*, with the same root as community and communion, implies a sharing among equals. Jesus allows no hierarchy of gifts here: the gifts of the rich are not of greater worth than the gifts of the poor, nor are those of the poor greater than those of the rich. Those of the scholar are not greater than those of the deckhand, nor are those of the bishop greater than those of the custodian. As children of the light, all have been given gifts for the common good. And all have their source in the light that has arisen upon us.

The light has come; we are now invited to shine. The glory of the Lord is risen upon us; it is now given to us to arise and follow. Christ has revealed his glory; we are called to welcome the transfiguring light of this love.

Praying in Epiphany

INVITATION

The Lord will arise upon you,
and his glory will appear over you.
Nations will come to your light,
and kings to the brightness of your dawn.
Isaiah 60:2b-3

TABLE PRAYER

O God of glory,
in the epiphany of your Son
light has dawned over the face of the earth.
Nourish us with this food and drink,
that your justice, peace, and truth
may be made known to all the world
through Christ our Lord. Amen

HYMN

Arise, your light has come! the Spirit's call obey;
show forth the glory of your God which shines on you today.

Arise, your light has come! Fling wide the prison door;
proclaim the captive's liberty, good tidings to the poor.

Arise your light has come! All you in sorrow born,
bind up the brokenhearted ones and comfort those who mourn.

Arise, your light has come! The mountains burst in song!
Rise up like eagles on the wing, God's pow'r will make us strong.
Tune: FESTAL SONG

PSALM 36:5-9

Your steadfast love, O Lord, extends to the heavens,
your faithfulness to the clouds.
Your righteousness is like the mighty mountains,
your judgments are like the great deep;
you save humans and animals alike, O Lord.

How precious is your steadfast love, O God!
    All people may take refuge in the shadow of your wings.
They feast on the abundance of your house,
    and you gave them to drink from the river of your delights.
For with you is the fountain of life;
    in your light we see light.

SCRIPTURE

See the daily readings

CANTICLE

In the morning, the Song of Zechariah (page 21)
In the evening, the Song of Mary (page 26)
At bedtime, the Song of Simeon (page 29) or

For Zion's sake I will not keep silent,
    and for Jerusalem's sake I will not rest,
until her vindication shines out like the dawn,
    and her salvation like a burning torch.

The nations shall see your vindication,
    and all the kings your glory;
and you shall be called by a new name
    that the mouth of the LORD will give.

You shall be a crown of beauty in the hand of the LORD,
    and a royal diadem in the hand of your God.

For as a young man marries a young woman,
    so shall your builder marry you,
and as the bridegroom rejoices over the bride,
    so shall your God rejoice over you.
      Isaiah 62:1-3, 5

PRAYER

Prayers for others and ourselves
The Lord's Prayer

Exalted God, you illumine the darkness with your light.
You shine forth with beauty and truth.
Bring to light all that is hidden.
Show forth your will and your power.
Make yourself known to your people,
and show us the way to justice and peace.
We ask this through Christ our Lord. Amen

BLESSING OF THE HOME

On the day of Epiphany, January 6, use a piece of chalk to mark the date and the initials of the Magi on the lintel of your home. Mark the first two numbers of the year and a † before the initials, the last two numbers after the initials. The finished inscription will read, for example, 19 † C † M † B † 98. The following blessing may be used:

O God our help in ages past,
our hope for years to come,
bless this house and all who enter through this door.
Make us ready to leave all behind and follow your light
as did your servants Caspar *(mark a C and a †),*
Melchior *(mark an M and a †),*
and Balthasar *(mark a B and a †).*
May we in this year
proclaim your everlasting glory
in a world troubled by fear and sin. Amen

THANKSGIVING FOR BAPTISM

Use this prayer on the Baptism of our Lord or whenever appropriate

O Holy One,
blessed are you in the Spirit hovering over the waters;
blessed are you in the Word going forth like gentle rain;
blessed are you in the baptism of Jesus at the Jordan;
blessed are you in our washing with water and the Holy Spirit;
blessed are you in every water that calls to mind our birth from the
 font;
blessed are you in the river of life that flows through the new
 Jerusalem;
blessed are you—Father, Son, and Holy Spirit—now and forever.
 Amen

PRAYERS FOR THE UNITY OF CHRISTIANS

*Use this prayer during the Week of Prayer for Christian Unity, the third week
in January*

Strong God of peace,
in the name of our Lord Jesus
and in the power of the Holy Spirit,
we commit ourselves to the service of your church.
Transform the ignorance that divides us,
fill our hearts with your love,
and give us one voice to offer you praise,
great and merciful God,
Father, Son, and Holy Spirit,
now and forever. Amen

BLESSING FOR CANDLEMAS/PRESENTATION OF OUR LORD

On February 2, the Presentation of the Lord, many Christians light candles in their homes in honor of Christ, the light (See Luke 2:22-40). Light a candle and say,

God of night and of day,
we praise you for the brightness of our sun,
for the softer light of the moon
and the splendor of the stars,
for the fires of earth that bring us light and warmth
even as they imperil all who use them.
By the great and small lights we mark our days and seasons,
we brighten the night and bring warmth to our winter,
and in these lights we see light:
Jesus, whose light we receive in baptism,
whose light we carry by day and by night.

In the beauty of these candles
keep us in quiet and in peace,
keep us safe and turn our hearts to you
that we may ourselves be light for our world.

All praise be yours through Christ,
the light of nations,
the glory of Israel,
for ever and ever. Amen

Daily Readings and Prayers

The Epiphany of our Lord

Jan. 6 Isa. 60:1-6   Ps. 72:1-7, 10-14
         Eph. 3:1-12   Matt 2:1-2
Jan. 7 Dan. 1:1-20   **Jan. 8** Dan. 2:17-23, 46-49
Jan. 9 Luke 1:67-79 **Jan. 10** Num. 24:15-19
Jan. 11 Eph. 4:17—5:1 **Jan. 12** Ps. 21

FOR PRAYER THROUGHOUT THE DAY

Lord, lead us with your light.
See Isaiah 60:2-3

A PRAYER FOR THE WEEK

God of glory,
your Son has revealed the light of your love.
Bless our days with the radiance of your grace
and guide us by the brightness of Christ, the morning star. Amen

The Baptism of our Lord

S Isa. 43:1-7   Ps. 29
     Acts 8:14-17   Luke 3:15-17, 21-22
M Judg. 4:1-10, 12-16 **T** Judg. 5:12-21
W Luke 11:33-36   **Th** Deut. 8:11-20
F I John 5:13-20   **S** Ps. 106:1-12

A PRAYER THROUGHOUT THE DAY

Do not fear, I have redeemed you.
See Isaiah 43:1

A PRAYER FOR THE WEEK

God our creator,
you have brought us to life in the waters of baptism.
Let us hear your Spirit's voice who says:
You are my beloved, with you I am well pleased. Amen

Second Sunday after the Epiphany

S   Isa. 62:1-5   Ps. 36:5-10
       I Cor. 12:1-11   John 2:1-11
M   Isa. 54:1-8   **T**   Jer. 3:19-23
W   Luke 5:33-40   **Th** Song of Sol. 4:9-5:1
F   I Cor. 1:4-17   **S**   Ps. 36

FOR PRAYER THROUGHOUT THE DAY

You are not forsaken, you are mine, says the Lord.
        See *Isaiah 62:4*

A PRAYER FOR THE WEEK

O God,
send your Spirit upon us that we may serve Christ,
the new wine poured out for the life of the world. Amen

Third Sunday after the Epiphany

S   Neh. 8:1-3, 5-6, 8-10   Ps. 19
       I Cor. 12:12-31a   Luke 4:14-21
M   Jer. 36:1-4, 20-26   **T**   Jer. 36:27-36
W   Luke 4:42-44   **Th** Isa. 61:1-7
F   I Cor. 14:1-12   **S**   Ps. 119:89-96

FOR PRAYER THROUGHOUT THE DAY

If one suffers, all suffer together.
        1 Corinthians 12:26

A PRAYER FOR THE WEEK

Lord Jesus,
you have anointed us with your Spirit
to bring good news to the poor.
Fix our eyes on you alone so that we may proclaim
your freedom for all who are oppressed. Amen

Fourth Sunday after the Epiphany

S	Jer. 1:4-10		Ps. 71:1-6
	1 Cor. 13:1-13		Luke 4:21-30
M	1 Kings 17:8-16	**T**	2 Kings 5:1-14
W	Luke 19:41-44	**Th**	Jer. 1:11-19
F	1 Cor. 14:13-25	**S**	Ps. 71

FOR PRAYER THROUGHOUT THE DAY

Lord, give me strength to speak your truth.
See *Jeremiah 1:9*

A PRAYER FOR THE WEEK

O Lord,
bring to maturity the gifts you have planted in us.
Water us with the rain of your Spirit
so that faith, hope, and love may flourish in us. Amen

Fifth Sunday after the Epiphany

S	Isa. 6:1-8 [9-13]		Ps. 138
	1 Cor. 15:1-11		Luke 5:1-11
M	1 Sam. 9:15—10:1a	**T**	2 Sam. 5:1-10
W	Luke 5:27-32	**Th**	Isa. 8:1-15
F	1 Cor. 14:26-40	**S**	Ps. 115

FOR PRAYER THROUGHOUT THE DAY

Here I am Lord. Send me to do your will.
See *Isaiah 6:8*

A PRAYER FOR THE WEEK

Good and gracious God,
when we are troubled and fearful,
hold us in the net of your mercy and peace. Amen

Sixth Sunday after the Epiphany

S   Jer. 17:5-10   Ps. 1
       1 Cor. 15:12-20   Luke 6:17-26
M   Isa. 3:9-17   **T**   Jer. 22:11-17
W Luke 11:37-52   **Th** Ezek. 24:1-14
F   1 Cor. 15:20-34   **S**   Ps. 120

FOR PRAYER THROUGHOUT THE DAY

Lord, search my heart and lead me in your way.
See *Jeremiah 17:10*

A PRAYER FOR THE WEEK

Merciful God,
you do not abandon the poor, the hungry, and the sorrowful.
Give us ready hearts to serve those
who call out for help. Amen

Seventh Sunday after the Epiphany

S   Gen. 45:3-11, 15   Ps. 37:1-11, 39-40
       1 Cor. 15:35-38, 42-50   Luke 6:27-38
M   Gen. 33:1-17   **T**   1 Sam. 24:1-22
W Luke 17:1-14   **Th** Lev. 5:1-13
F   1 Cor. 15:35-43   **S**   Ps. 38

FOR PRAYER THROUGHOUT THE DAY

O Lord, be merciful to me a sinner.
See *Luke 6:37*

A PRAYER FOR THE WEEK

Merciful God,
teach us to love our enemies and
to forgive those who sin against us
for the sake of Christ our Lord. Amen

Eighth Sunday after the Epiphany

S	Isa. 55:10-13		Ps. 92:1-4, 12-15
	I Cor. 15:51-58		Luke 6:39-49
M	Jer. 24:1-10	**T**	Jer. 29:10-18
W	Luke 14:34-35	**Th**	Prov. 5:1-23
F	I Cor. 16:1-24	**S**	Ps. I

FOR PRAYER THROUGHOUT THE DAY

Prepare my heart to receive your word.
See *Isaiah 55:10*

A PRAYER FOR THE WEEK

Come to us, O God,
in times of trouble and fear
and be our refuge and strength. Amen

Transfiguration

S	Exod. 34:29-35		Ps. 99
	2 Cor. 3:12-4		Luke 9:28-36 [37-43]
M	Ezek .1:1-2:1	**T**	Luke 10:21-24

FOR PRAYER THROUGHOUT THE DAY

Lord of glory, let your light illumine our path.

A PRAYER FOR THE WEEK

Holy God,
open our ears to hear Christ's voice
that we may follow him as faithful disciples. Amen

Lent

Return to the Lord, your God, for he is gracious and merciful, slow to anger, and abounding in steadfast love. Joel 2:13

With these words, the people of God are called to be attentive to the Word of God. With these words, the church announces that something is different about these days: it is Lent, and the people of God have embarked on the path of return for forty days.

Repentance, turn, return—in Hebrew all three words have a common root. Lent has a character of turning away from those things that usually preoccupy us and of moving in another direction, as Jesus did when he entered the wilderness. It is a turning away from those things that oppress and dominate us, as Israel did in leaving Egypt. It is a turning away from all that prevents us from sensing and living in the steadfast love of God. And, as it was for Israel and Jesus, it is a path into wilderness.

In life's wilderness—in times of doubt, illness, sorrow, loss—the temptations to question the loving presence of God are many. The temptation to place one's loyalty with the immediately gratifying but false gods of power, wealth, and fame is strong. So for the forty days of Lent we take the path that leads through the wilderness. We take on simple disciplines—prayer, fasting, acts of love—to show our willingness to take in the deeper discipline of turning from all those things that can separate us from God.

We fast as a sign of our willingness to set boundaries for ourselves. We fast as a sign of our connection to all those whose daily lives are filled with hunger. We pray for forgive-ness, for right relationship—with ourselves, with others, with creation, with God. We do acts of charity and kindness to begin living out the return for which we pray.

For these reasons the season of Lent begins with ashes: the residue of burning, the leaving behind of binding things; a sign of humility, as in human, humus, humble; a sign of mourning for sin, separation, or lost life; a sign of repentance and turning to the only One who can lead us from the ashes and dust of the grave to the feast of eternal life.

It is also why Lent begins with confession, a conscious, voluntary examination of how we have separated ourselves from God and each other. With the words, "We confess," we join others in a united plea for mercy. We support one another in our confession because we know that sin affects the entire community. Then for forty days—the time of Israel in the wilderness, of Moses on the mountain, of Jesus in the desert—we are given the chance to name that which separates us from God and to pray for healing and reconcilia-tion. We are given this gracious time in which to repent, to turn around and go in the opposite direction. We are given forty days to turn away, to turn around, to return.

God waits constantly and steadfastly for our return. Each day, each season, of the church year is but a microcosm, a condensation, a distillation of the truths God has revealed through his word. The church year is simply an opportunity for us to remember rather than forget, to participate rather than observe, to live rather than simply think about our life in Christ. God is always God-with-us, not just at Christmas, but at Christmas we call this to mind. We are always in need of repentance, and God always awaits our return, not just in Lent, but in Lent we consciously call this to mind.

So at the center of this year's cycle of scripture readings we hear a parable from Jesus, the story of the return of the prodigal son. Prodigal—wasteful and extravagant, a wasted life, wasted relationship, wasted treasure, wasted inheritance—yet all to be forgiven by the faithful and truly prodigal father, who desires only return.

"The word is very near you," says the LORD. Interestingly, not so that you can hear it, not so that you can think about it, but "so that you can do it" (Deut. 30:14; Rom. 10:8). Returning to God is not a mental exercise, but a turn that changes the very way a person lives. "I am about to do a new thing; now it springs forth, do you not perceive it? I will make a way in the wilderness and rivers in the desert" (Isa. 43:19).

The path into the desert also leads out of the desert. Paul writes: "God is faithful, and he will not let you be tested beyond your strength, but with the testing he will also provide a way out so that you may be able to endure it" (1 Cor. 10:13). At the other end of this dry and austere path there is Jesus, a ministering angel; for Israel, freedom; for the baptismal candidate, water and rebirth; for the Lenten wanderer, forgiveness. At the other end of this desert way is an ending, which is a beginning. What was lost has returned with shouts of joy.

Praying in Lent

INVITATION

Return to the LORD, your God,
for he is gracious and merciful,
slow to anger, and abounding in steadfast love.
Joel 2:13

TABLE PRAYER

O LORD our God, maker of all things,
through your goodness you have blessed us
with the gifts of this table.
Turn our hearts toward you and
toward all those in need.
Guide us on our Lenten journey
and bring us to the joy of Easter
through Christ our Lord. Amen

HYMN

O Sun of justice, Jesus Christ,
dispel the darkness of our hearts,
till your blest light makes nighttime flee
and brings the joys your day imparts.

In this our "time acceptable"
touch ev'ry heart with sorrow, Lord,
that, turned from sin, renewed by grace,
we may press on toward love's reward.

The day, your day, in beauty dawns
when in your light earth blooms anew;
led back again to life's true way,
may we, forgiv'n, rejoice in you.

O loving Trinity, our God,
to you we bow through endless days,
and in your grace new-born we sing
new hymns of gratitude and praise.
Tune: JESUS DULCIS MEMORIA

PSALM 126

When the LORD restored the fortunes of Zion,
  we were like those who dream.
Then our mouth was filled with laughter,
  and our tongue with shouts of joy;
then it was said among the nations,
  "The LORD has done great things for them."
The LORD has done great things for us,
  and we rejoiced.

Restore our fortunes, O LORD,
  like the watercourses of the Negeb.
May those who sow in tears
  reap with shouts of joy.
Those who go out weeping,
  bearing the seed for sowing,
shall come home with shouts of joy,
  carrying their sheaves.

SCRIPTURE

See the daily readings

CANTICLE

In the morning, the Song of Zechariah (page 21)
In the evening, the Song of Mary (page 26)
At bedtime, the Song of Simeon (page 29) or

Christ Jesus, who though he was in the form of God,
did not regard equality with God
as something to be exploited,
but emptied himself,
taking the form of a slave,
being born in human likeness.

And being found in human form,
he humbled himself
and became obedient to the point of death—
even death on a cross.

Therefore God also highly exalted him
and gave him the name
that is above every name,

so that at the name of Jesus
every knee should bend,
in heaven and on earth and under the earth,
and every tongue should confess
that Jesus Christ is Lord
to the glory of the Father.
Philippians 2:6-11

PRAYER

Prayers for others and ourselves
The Lord's Prayer

From all desires that part us from you
 turn us, O God,
from deceit and illusion
 protect us, O God.
From all our wayward and selfish ways
 deliver us, O God.
To the joy of your salvation
 restore us, O God.
To a right spirit
 convert us, O God.
To your waiting arms
 return us, O God. Amen

Lord, have mercy.
Christ, have mercy.
Lord, have mercy.
O Christ hear us.
 In mercy hear us.

By the mystery of your incarnation:
 Help us, good Lord.
By your holy birth:
 Help us, good Lord.
By your baptism:
 Help us, good Lord.

By your fasting and temptation:
>Help us, good Lord.
By your agony:
>Help us, good Lord.
By your cross and suffering:
>Help us, good Lord.
By your resurrection:
>Help us, good Lord.
By your ascension:
>Help us, good Lord.
By the gift of the Holy Spirit:
>Help us, good Lord.
Lamb of God, you take away the sin of the world;
>have mercy on us.
Lamb of God, you take away the sin of the world;
>have mercy on us.
Lamb of God, you take away the sin of the world;
>grant us peace.

BLESSING FOR THE LENTEN SEASON

Use this blessing to begin your prayer time during the season of Lent

God of mercy,
as we move through the journey of this season
incite us to truthful reflection, faithful action,
and quiet release of all that is false and fleeting.
Deliver us from every evil and protect us from all anxiety
as we wait in joyful hope for the great feast of Easter,
the passover of the Lord Jesus from death to life with you. Amen

BLESSING FOR ALMS AND FASTING

Use this reading and prayer as you begin the Lenten disciplines of prayer, almsgiving, and fasting

Do not be afraid, little flock,
for it is your Father's good pleasure to give you the kingdom.
Sell your possessions, and give alms.
Make purses for yourselves that do not wear out,
an unfailing treasure in heaven,
where no thief comes near and no moth destroys.
For where your treasure is, there your heart will be also.
Luke 12:32-34

Loving God,
you ask us to seek heavenly treasures.
Consecrate these forty days for prayer
that our spirits may hear your voice.
Consecrate these forty days for fasting
that our bodies may learn wisdom and compassion.
Consecrate these forty days to acts of love
that our neighbors may know your blessing,
through Christ our Lord
who walked this wilderness before us. Amen

THANKSGIVING FOR THE CROSS

Use this prayer before a cross or image of the crucified Lord

Holy God,
Holy and Mighty,
Holy Immortal One,
have mercy upon us.
The Trisagion

PRAYER FOR PLACING PALMS IN THE HOME

Use this blessing when placing palms in the home following the Palm Sunday liturgy. The palms may be placed in a place of prayer in the home or behind icons and holy images.

Blessed is the One who comes in the name of the Lord!
May we who place these palms receive Christ into our midst
with the joy that marked the entrance to Jerusalem.
May we hold no betrayal in our hearts,
but peacefully welcome Christ
who lives and reigns with you and the Holy Spirit,
one God, now and forever. Amen

Daily Reading and Prayers

 ## Ash Wednesday

W Joel 2:1-2, 12-17   Ps. 51:1-17
2 Cor. 5:20b—6:10   Matt. 6:1-6, 16-21
Th Exod. 5:10-23   **F** Exod. 6:1-13
S Eccles. 3:1-8

FOR PRAYER THROUGHOUT THE DAY

Have mercy on me, O God.
Psalm 51:1

A PRAYER FOR THE WEEK

Good and gracious God,
create in me a clean heart
and renew your spirit within me.
Restore to me the joy of your salvation. Amen

First Sunday in Lent

S Deut. 26:1-11   Ps. 91:1-2, 9-16
Rom. 10:8b-13   Luke 4:1-13
M 1 Chron. 21:1-17   **T** Zech. 3:1-10
W Luke. 22:1-6   **Th** Jer. 9:18—10:3
F Rom. 3:9-22a   **S** Ps. 91

FOR PRAYER THROUGHOUT THE DAY

O God, my refuge, in you alone I place my trust.
Psalm 91:2

A PRAYER FOR THE WEEK

God our redeemer,
guide us through this life with your word
and when we fall, raise us up and restore us
through Christ our Lord. Amen

Second Sunday in Lent

S Gen. 15:1-12, 17-18   Ps. 27
    Phil. 3:17—4:1   Luke 13:31-35
M Exod. 33:1-6   **T** Lev. 26:23-26, 40-45
W Luke 13:22-30   **Th** 2 Chron. 20:1-23
F Rom. 4:1-12   **S** Ps. 105

FOR PRAYER THROUGHOUT THE DAY

The Lord is my help; whom shall I fear?
Psalm 27:1

A PRAYER FOR THE WEEK

As a mother holds and protects her children,
so gather us into your merciful arms, O God.
Make us strong in faith
so that we may be your witnesses in the world. Amen

Third Sunday in Lent

S Isa. 55:1-9   Ps. 63:1-8
    1 Cor. 10:1-13   Luke 13:1-9
M Jer. 11:1-17   **T** Ezek. 17:1-10
W Luke 13:18-21   **Th** Num. 13:17-27
F Rom. 2:1-16   **S** Ps. 63

FOR PRAYER THROUGHOUT THE DAY

O God, my soul thirsts for you.
Psalm 63:1

A PRAYER FOR THE WEEK

Ever-faithful God,
you do not test us beyond our strength.
Keep us steadfast in your word
and bring forth good fruit in our lives. Amen

Fourth Sunday in Lent

S	Josh. 5:9-12		Ps. 32
	2 Cor. 5:16-21		Luke 15:1-3, 11b-32
M	Lev. 23:26-32	**T**	Lev. 25:1-19
W	Luke 9:10-17	**Th**	Isa. 25:6-10
F	Rev. 19:1-9	**S**	Ps. 14

FOR PRAYER THROUGHOUT THE DAY

You are a hiding place for me.
Psalm 32:7

A PRAYER FOR THE WEEK

As deep as the sea
and as high as the heavens
is your mercy, O God.
With the power of your Spirit,
forgive us, heal us, and make us strong. Amen

Fifth Sunday in Lent

S	Isa. 43:16-21		Ps. 126
	Phil. 3:4b-14		John 12:1-8
M	Exod. 40:1-15	**T**	Judg. 9:7-15
W	Luke 18:31-34	**Th**	Hab. 3:1-15
F	1 John 2:18-27	**S**	Ps. 20

FOR PRAYER THROUGHOUT THE DAY

The LORD has done great things for us.
Psalm 126:3

A PRAYER FOR THE WEEK

Lord Jesus,
you came among us not to be served
but to serve those in need.
Keep us faithful in your service
and strengthen us to be ministers of forgiveness. Amen

Holy Week

Passion Sunday
    Isa. 50:4-9a
    Phil. 2:5-11
M Heb. 9:11-15
W John 13:21-32

    Luke 19:28-40
    Ps. 31:9-16
    Luke 22:14—23:56
T John 12:20-36

FOR PRAYER THROUGHOUT THE DAY

Though he was in the form of God,
Jesus became obedient to death, death on the cross.
Philippians 2:6,8

A PRAYER FOR THE WEEK

Merciful God,
send your Spirit upon us
and prepare our hearts to celebrate
Christ's passover from death to eternal life with you. Amen

Three Days

Have this mind among yourselves, which is yours in Christ Jesus, who though he was in the form of God, did not count equality with God a thing to be grasped, but emptied himself, taking the form of a servant. Philippians 2:6

From the beginning of the Maundy Thursday liturgy, we are met with an intensity unlike that of any other time in the year. We have come to the turning point of the year, the great Three Days that gather into themselves the central matters of hunger and nourishment, freedom and slavery, life and death, God and humanity. Here we experience the service and sacrifice of the Lord Jesus and, through him, encounter the fundamental Christian interpretation of all life.

During Lent we have undertaken the wilderness path of renewal, a turning toward God: a path of examination, of truthfulness, of repentance. On Maundy Thursday, we are declared a forgiven people. Then, a most unusual action takes place—we see the washing of common, ordinary feet. It is startling enough to cause a child to ask, "Why, on this day, do we wash people's feet?" And we answer: "Because on this day our Lord Jesus gave us the commandment to love one another as he has loved us." A loving service is the life we are to live as forgiven people. The bowl, the towel, the kneeling Jesus attest to it; the commandment confirms it; Jesus' life exemplifies it. "O Lord, I am your servant," we sing in Psalm 116. "Wash one another's feet," Jesus says in John's gospel, "love one another."

The forgiven person is willing to kneel for people, to honor the most humble of tasks, to sacrifice for the good of others. It is a different way of living one's life in our contemporary world. And the motivating force behind such sacrifice is love.

The forgiven life is a life of connections, initiated by the bath called baptism and nourished by the meal called communion. By eating together at the Lord's table, we are challenged to become what we have consumed: the body of Christ—united with God, with Christ, with the saints, united with each other and with all creation.

The life of a servant is above all a life of sacrifice, as made known in the sacrificial love of Jesus, and symbolized by the elements of the holy supper. By eating the bread, we are nourished by sacrifice just as the many grains of wheat in relinquishing themselves become something new together. By drinking the wine, we are nourished by another's suffering love just as the grapes in being crushed become something new. "As often as we eat of this bread and drink of this cup, we proclaim the Lord's death until he comes."

As the Maundy Thursday liturgy closes, as we move into Good Friday, the scriptures announce that in Jesus' suffering and death on the cross, creation is shaken to the very core: the skies darken, the earth quakes, graves open. And significantly, the veil of the temple is torn in two from top to bottom. That which separated humans from God is entirely, irreparably, torn. Defeat yields to victory. Sacrifice yields to thanksgiving. And the power of the cross is revealed.

This paradox of sacrifice and triumph is beautifully interwoven in Psalm 22, spoken from the cross by the suffering Christ, sung at the close of the Maundy Thursday liturgy and again on Good Friday. The psalm begins in lament and ends with praise. The psalmist understands that in the darkness of this suffering is the spark of God's promise: even if one cannot yet see it, the psalmist sings praise.

That spark of promise enters the darkness on the third day at the Vigil of Easter. The spark enters and flames into the new fire and the paschal candle. It is new light, light triumphant, but with the mark of five wounds. And here the paradox of sacrifice: as the light from the candle is divided and shared among the faithful present in the darkened church, it becomes brighter, not dim. "We sing the glories of this pillar of fire, the brightness of which is not diminished, even when its light is divided and borrowed." As the light is shared, it spreads and illumines all. The power unleashed by the death of Christ overturns all normal expectations. There is light in the darkness; in sacrifice, abundance; in servanthood, power; in death, life.

Therefore God also highly exalted him and gave him the name that is above every name, so that at the name of Jesus every knee should bend in heaven and on earth and under the earth. Phillipians 2:9

Praying in the Three Days

INVITATION

Christ became obedient unto death—
even death on a cross.
Therefore God highly exalted him
and gave him the name that is above every name.
Philippians 2:8-9

TABLE PRAYER

We bless you, O God,
for this food that strengthens us
on our journey from death to life.
As we celebrate the Lord's passover,
hold us in your mercy and raise us at last
with Christ to the joy of the resurrection. Amen

BLESSING FOR THE THREE DAYS

Use this prayer to begin your prayer time during the Three Days

God of our salvation,
your word does not return to you empty,
but accomplishes your good and holy purposes.
May all blessing and honor be yours
for these great three days
in which the healing of the nations was set forth,
and the salvation of the world arose. Amen

Maundy Thursday

HYMN

Where charity and love prevail, there God is ever found;
brought here together by Christ's love, by love we thus are bound.

With grateful joy and holy fear, God's charity we learn;
let us with heart and mind and soul now love God in return.

Let us recall that in our midst dwells Christ, God's holy Son;
as members of each body joined, in him we are made one.

Tune: TWENTY-FOURTH

PSALM 34: 1-6, 8-10

I will bless the LORD at all times;
 his praise shall continually be in my mouth.
My soul shall makes its boast in the LORD;
 let the humble hear and be glad.
O magnify the LORD with me,
 and let us exalt his name.

I sought the LORD, and he answered me,
 and delivered me from all my fears.
Look to him and be radiant;
 so your faces shall never be ashamed.
This poor soul cried, and was heard by the LORD,
 and was saved from every trouble.

O taste and see that the LORD is good;
 happy are those who take refuge in him.
O fear the LORD, you his holy ones,
 for those who fear him have no want.
The young lions suffer want and hunger,
 but those who seek the LORD lack no good thing.

SCRIPTURE

Exod. 12:1-14	Ps. 116
1 Cor. 11:23-26	John 13:1-17, 31-35

CANTICLE

If I speak in the tongues of mortals and angels,
but do not have love, I am a noisy gong or a clanging symbol.
And if I have prophetic powers,
and understand all mysteries and all knowledge,
and if I have all faith, so as to remove mountains,
but do not have love, I am nothing.
If I give away all my possessions,
and if I hand over my body so that I may boast,
but do not have love, I gain nothing.

Love is patient; love is kind;
love is not envious or boastful or arrogant or rude.
It does not insist on its own way;
it is not irritable or resentful;
it does not rejoice in wrongdoing, but rejoices in the truth.
It bears all things, believes all things, hopes all things,
endures all things.

Love never ends.
But as for prophecies, they will come to an end;
as for tongues; they will cease;
as for knowledge, it will come to an end.
For we know only in part and we prophesy only in part;
but when the complete comes, the partial will come to an end.

When I was a child,
I spoke like a child, I thought like a child, I reasoned like a child;
when I became an adult, I put an end to childish ways.
For now we see in a mirror, dimly,
but then we will see face to face.
Now I know only in part; then I will know fully,
even as I have been fully known.

And now faith, hope, and love abide, these three;
and the greatest of these is love.
1 Corinthians 13

PRAYER

Prayers for others and ourselves
The Lord's Prayer

Holy God, source of all love,
on the night of his betrayal,
Jesus gave his disciples a new commandment:
To love one another as he loved them.
By your Holy Spirit, write this commandment in our hearts;
through your Son, Jesus Christ our Lord,
who lives and reigns with you and the Holy Spirit,
one God, now and forever. Amen

Good Friday

HYMN

Were you there when they crucified my Lord?
Were you there when they crucified my Lord?
Oh, sometimes it causes me to tremble, tremble, tremble.
Were you there when they crucified my Lord?

Were you there when they nailed him to the tree?
Were you there when they nailed him to the tree?
Oh, sometimes it causes me to tremble, tremble, tremble.
Were you there when they nailed him to the tree?

Were you there when they laid him in the tomb?
Were you there when they laid him in the tomb?
Oh, sometimes it causes me to tremble, tremble, tremble.
Were you there when they laid him in the tomb?

Were you there when God raised him from the tomb?
Were you there when God raised him from the tomb?
Oh, sometimes it causes me to tremble, tremble, tremble.
Were you there when God raised him from the tomb?
Tune: WERE YOU THERE

PSALM 22:22-24, 27-31

I will tell of your great name to my brothers and sisters;
   in the midst of the congregation I will praise you:
You who fear the LORD, praise him!
   All you offspring of Jacob, glorify him;
   stand in awe of him, all you offspring of Israel!
For he did not despise or abhor
   the affliction of the afflicted;
he did not hide his face from me,
   but heard when I cried to him.

All the ends of the earth shall remember
   and turn to the LORD;
and all the families of the nations
   shall worship before him.
For dominion belongs to the LORD,
   and he rules over the nations.

To him, indeed shall all who sleep in the earth bow down,
   before him shall bow all who go down to the dust,
   and I shall live for him.
Posterity will serve him;
   future generations will be told about the LORD,
   and proclaim his deliverance to a people yet unborn,
   saying that he has done it.

SCRIPTURE

Isa. 52:13-53:12   Ps. 22
Heb. 10:16-25   John 18:1-19:42

CANTICLE

Christ also suffered for you,
leaving you an example,
so that you should follow in his steps.

He committed no sin
and no deceit was found in his mouth.
When he was abused, he did not return abuse;
when he suffered, he did not threaten;
but he entrusted himself to the one who judges justly.

He himself bore our sins in his body on the cross,
so that free from sins, we might live for righteousness;
by his wounds you have been healed.
1 Peter 2:21-24

PRAYER

Prayers for others and ourselves
The Lord's Prayer

Almighty God,
your Son Jesus Christ was lifted high upon the cross
so that he might draw the whole world to himself.
Grant that we who glory in his death for our salvation
may also glory in his call to take up our cross and follow him;
through your Son, Jesus Christ our Lord,
who lives and reigns with you and the Holy Spirit,
one God, now and forever. Amen

Behold, the life-giving cross
on which was hung the salvation of the whole world.
We adore you, O Christ, and we bless you.
By your holy cross you have redeemed the world.

The Vigil of Easter

HYMN

We know that Christ is raised and dies no more.
Embraced by death, he broke its fearful hold,
and our despair he turned to blazing joy. Hallelujah!

We share by water in his saving death.
Reborn, we share with him an Easter life,
as living members of our Savior Christ. Hallelujah!

The Father's splendor clothes the Son with life.
The Spirit's fission shakes the Church of God.
Baptized, we live with God the Three in One. Hallelujah!

A new creation comes to life and grows
as Christ's new body takes on flesh and blood
The universe restored and whole will sing: Hallelujah!
Tune: ENGLEBERG

PSALM 118:5-9, 14

Out of my distress I called on the LORD;
 the LORD answered me and set me in a broad place.
With the LORD on my side I do not fear.
 What can mortals do to me?
The LORD is on my side to help me;
 I shall look in triumph on those who hate me.
It is better to take refuge in the LORD
 than to put confidence in mortals.
It is better to take refuge in the LORD
 than to put confidence in princes.
The LORD is my strength and my might;
 he has become my salvation.

SCRIPTURE

Gen. 1:1-2:4a	Gen. 7:1-9:17	Gen. 22:1-18
Exod. 14:10-31; 15:2-21	Isa. 55:1-11	Prov. 8:1-9:6
Ezek. 36:24-28	Ezek. 37:1-14	Zeph. 3:14-20
Rom. 6:3-11	Ps. 114	Luke 24:1-12

CANTICLE

I will sing to the LORD,
for he has triumphed gloriously;
horse and rider he has thrown into the sea.

The LORD is my strength and my might,
and he has become my salvation;
this is my God, and I will praise him,
my father's God, and I will exalt him.

The LORD is a warrior;
the LORD is his name.
Pharaoh's chariots and his army he cast into the sea;
his picked officers were sunk in the Red Sea.
The floods covered them;
they went down into the depths like a stone.

Your right hand, O LORD, glorious in power—
your right, O LORD, shattered the enemy.

Who is like you, O LORD, among the gods?
Who is like you, majestic in holiness,
awesome in splendor, doing wonders?
You stretched out your right hand, the earth swallowed them.

In your steadfast love you led the people who you redeemed;
you guided them by your strength to your holy abode.

You brought them in
and planted them on the mountain of your possession,
the place, O LORD, that you made your abode,
the sanctuary, O LORD, that your hands have established.
The LORD will reign forever and ever.
Exodus 15:1-6, 11-13, 17-18

PRAYER

Prayers for others and ourselves
The Lord's Prayer

O God,
who made this most holy night
to shine with the glory of the Lord's resurrection:
Stir up in your church that Spirit of adoption
which is given to us in baptism,
that being renewed both in body and mind,
we may worship you in sincerity and truth. Amen

Almighty and everlasting God,
in the mystery of the dying and rising of Christ
you established a new covenant of reconciliation.
Cleanse our hearts and give a new spirit to your people,
that all those reborn in Baptism
may show forth in their lives what they profess by faith;
through your Son, Jesus Christ our Lord. Amen

May the light of Christ, rising in glory,
dispel the darkness of our hearts and minds. Amen

Easter

*I*t is the first Sunday after the first full moon after the spring equinox. It is the last remnant of the lunar calendar in the Christian year. Newness is in the air. As the first rays of the rising sun race across the land, fear and darkness fade, uncertainty lifts up its face, sorrow becomes radiant. A day unlike any other day has dawned. The whole earth is illumined by the risen Son. It is Easter.

"See, I am making all things new," says the voice from the throne. All things new. Not just for one day, but for fifty days we celebrate the beginning of all things being made new. Fifty—a week of weeks: seven times seven, plus one great pentecostal day. Fifty—the number of days between the Jewish festivals of Passover and Pentecost (the fiftieth day). A celebration of completion: all that is necessary for God's reign to come has been set in motion.

In his first letter to the Corinthians, Paul describes Christ as "the first fruits of those who have died." The first fruits are the first of the planting to ripen, which are dedicated to and belong to God, as does the first of everything. The first fruits point to the continuing harvest of plantings. All that is necessary for completion has been set in motion.

The dawning on Easter Day is an ending and a beginning: I am the Alpha and the Omega, says the Lord, the beginning and the end. It is an ending of the fear of death and the grasping and clutching, which are its children. It is an ending of separation from God, for the veil of the temple is torn, and we hear these words: "The home of God is among mortals." It is the beginning of completion, of shalom, peace, wholeness, the light for which we longed in Advent. It is the beginning of the Spirit's power breathed into all without discrimination.

Pentecost, the final day of Easter, is the festival of the Spirit's power. As the Jewish Pentecost was a feast of the first fruits of the wheat harvest and later the first fruits of the covenant—the giving of the Ten Commandments—so the Christian Pentecost is a festival of first fruits of the promised Holy Spirit. Jesus said, "I am going away and I am coming to you." Like the burning bush Moses encountered, those inflamed with the Holy Spirit burned with tongues of flame above them, but were not consumed. "The home of God is among mortals." The sign of God's continuing presence is to be God's dwelling among mortals in the inspired lives of those transformed by the fire of the Spirit. All that is necessary for God's reign to come has been set in motion.

The light of the rising Son, the transforming fire of the Holy Spirit, these are gifts released by the sacrificial death of Christ. Fire cleanses, fire destroys, fire changes, fire ascends. The baptism of fire prophesied by John the Baptist and claimed by Jesus has its fruition in the pentecostal fire. The people are inspired, inspirited, breathed into by the rushing wind of the Spirit. Disciples now preach, followers now lead, the sick now heal, the blind now see visions, and mourners now raise the dead.

But these first fruits of the Spirit point to a continued harvest of like planting. Those who love God become the dwelling place of God. Not just in the first but also in the twentieth century. Not just for the white-robed martyrs, but for contemporary disciples.

A new day dawned on that springtime morn, a day of
God's completing, a day of revealing, a day of making things
new, and that day has not yet set.

Can there be any day but this,
Though many suns to shine endeavor?
We count three hundred, but we miss:
There is but one, and that one ever.
    George Herbert, "Easter"

Praying in Easter

INVITATION

The one who was seated on the throne said,
"See, I am making all things new."
Revelation 21:6

TABLE PRAYER

O Christ, the lamb of God,
by your passion, death, and resurrection,
you have brought salvation to the world.
Receive our thankful praise as we gather at this table
and nourish us on our paschal journey from death to eternal life.
you live and reign forever and ever. Amen

HYMN

Now the green blade rises from the buried grain,
wheat that in dark earth many days has lain;
Love lives again, that with the dead has been;
Love is come again like wheat arising green.

In the grave they laid him, love by hatred slain,
thinking that he would never wake again;
laid in the earth like grain that sleeps unseen;
Love is come again like wheat arising green.

Forth he came at Easter, like the risen grain,
he that for three days in the grave had lain;
raised from the dead, my living Lord is seen;
Love is come again like wheat arising green.

When our hearts are wintry, grieving, or in pain,
your touch can call us back to life again,
fields of our hearts that dead and bare have been;
Love is come again like wheat arising green.
Tune: NOEL NOUVELET

PSALM 118:19-24

Open to me the gates of righteousness,
that I may enter through them
and give thanks to the LORD.

This is the gate of the LORD;
the righteous shall enter through it.
I thank you that you have answered me
and become my salvation.
The stone that the builders rejected
has become the chief cornerstone.
This is the LORD's doing;
it is marvelous in our eyes.
This is the day that the LORD has made;
let us rejoice and be glad in it.

SCRIPTURE

See the daily readings

CANTICLE

Holy, holy, holy LORD, God of power and might.
Heaven and earth are full of your glory.
Hosanna in the highest!
Blessed is he who comes in the name of the LORD.
Hosanna in the highest!
Isaiah 6:3; Psalm 118:26

PRAYER

Prayers for others and ourselves
The Lord's Prayer

Almighty God,
through your only Son you overcame death
and opened for us the gate of everlasting life.
Give us your continual help;
lift us when we fall,
and fill us with the power of the resurrection,
that we may join with the whole creation in saying,
"Heaven and earth are full of your glory."
Grant this through Christ, our risen Lord. Amen

THANKSGIVING FOR BAPTISM DURING EASTER

Use this prayer throughout the Fifty Days of Easter. Gather around a bowl of water with a burning candle set next to it.

We give you praise, O God,
that in baptism you have led us from the night of sin
to the dawning of a new day.
We give you praise that, buried with Christ in baptism,
we too shall rise with him and walk in the light as your children.
Receive our praise through Jesus Christ,
    the resurrection and the life,
who lives and reigns with you and the Holy Spirit,
one God, now and forever. Amen

BLESSING OF THE EASTER MEAL

Use this reading and prayer before your first meal on Easter

On this mountain the Lord of hosts
will make for all peoples
a feast of rich food, a feast of well-aged wines,
of rich food filled with marrow, of well-aged wines strained clear.
And he will destroy on this mountain
the shroud that is cast over all peoples,
the sheet that is spread over all nations;
he will swallow up death forever.
    Isaiah 26:6-7

O Lord our God, creator of the universe,
we praise with greater joy than ever on this day
as we celebrate your triumph over the power of death.
You prepare a rich feast and invite the hungry to your table.
Bless us and this food of our first Easter meal
which we have received from your goodness.
Strengthen us in faith and lead us to the heavenly banquet,
through Christ our Lord. Amen

BLESSING OF THE HOME

Use this prayer when moving into a new dwelling

Peace be to this house:
  the peace of the God of the morning stars,
  the peace of the still small voice.
Peace be within these walls:
  the peace of the risen Christ,
  the peace of the five wounds.
Peace to all who enter here:
  the peace of the Spirit's holy fire,
  the peace of a loving hearth.
May the peace of Christ rule in our hearts,
now and forever. Amen

BLESSING OF FIELDS AND GARDENS

Use this prayer when preparing soil and planting

O God of all green and growing things,
from your hand flourish the riches of the earth.
Prosper the work of our hands
as we cultivate and tend the fertile soil.
Grant us hearts grateful
for the rain, the sun, the soil, the seed,
that we may touch the earth with wisdom
and use its gifts to your honor.
Grant this through Christ our Lord. Amen

BLESSING FOR MOTHER'S DAY

Use this prayer on the second Sunday in May

Under your wings, O Lord, you have held us,
as a mother holds her young.
Look with favor on all those women
who have sheltered children in their loving care.
Guide that they may lead;
strengthen that they may be tender;
grant wisdom that the people may live;
and hold all in your loving gaze
until we see you face to face. Amen

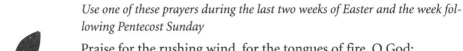

THANKSGIVING FOR THE HOLY SPIRIT

Use one of these prayers during the last two weeks of Easter and the week following Pentecost Sunday

Praise for the rushing wind, for the tongues of fire, O God;
praise for the visions, the sighs, the prayers;
praise for the power from on high;
praise for the Spirit, blessed gift. Amen

O Spirit of God, seek us;
Good Spirit, pray with us;
Spirit of counsel, inform us;
Spirit of might, free us;
Spirit of truth, enlighten us;
Spirit of Christ, raise us;
O Holy Spirit, dwell in us. Amen

Daily Readings and Prayers

Resurrection of the Lord

S	Acts 10:34-43 or Isa. 65:17-25		Ps. 118:1-2, 14-24
	1 Cor. 15:19-26		John 20:1-18
M	Josh. 10:16-27	T	2 Sam. 6:1-15
W	Luke 24:1-12	Th	Judg. 4:17-23; 5:24-31a
F	Rev. 12:1-12	S	Ps. 108

FOR PRAYER THROUGHOUT THE DAY

The LORD is my strength.
Psalm 118:14

A PRAYER FOR THE WEEK

Lord Jesus,
clear away our cloudy vision
so that we might see you risen from the grave
and know your abiding presence with us. Amen. Alleluia.

Second Sunday of Easter

S	Acts 5:27-32		Ps. 118:14-29
	Rev. 1:4-8		John 20:19-31
M	1 Sam. 17:1-11	T	1 Sam. 17:31-51
W	Luke 12:4-23	Th	Esther 8:1-17
F	Rev. 1:9-18	S	Ps. 144

FOR PRAYER THROUGHOUT THE DAY

When I am locked in fear, O Christ, give me your peace.
See *John 20:19*

A PRAYER FOR THE WEEK

We walk by faith, O God, and not by sight.
Come to us and lead us by the light of your word.
Hold us in the midst of our doubts
and guide us with your promises. Amen

Third Sunday of Easter

S Acts 9:1-6 [7-20] Ps. 30
  Rev. 5:11-14   John 21:1-19
M Acts 12:1-19 **T** Acts 26:1, 12-29
W Luke 5:1-11 **Th** Acts 11:19-30
F Rev. 5:1-10   **S** Ps. 143

FOR PRAYER THROUGHOUT THE DAY

> All blessing and honor and glory to you, Lord Jesus Christ.
> See *Revelation 5:12*

A PRAYER FOR THE WEEK

> God our shepherd,
> feed us with your word that we may follow Christ
> and serve your people in love. Amen

Fourth Sunday of Easter

S Acts 9:36-43 Ps. 23
  Rev. 7:9-17   John 10:22-30
M Jer. 50:17-20 **T** Ezek. 37:15-28
W John 10:31-42 **Th** Ezek. 45:1-9
F Rev. 6:1-7:3   **S** Ps. 23

FOR PRAYER THROUGHOUT THE DAY

> I fear no evil, O LORD, for you are with me.
> *Psalm 23:4*

A PRAYER FOR THE WEEK

> O Lord Jesus,
> open our ears to hear your voice
> so that we may follow you through this life
> until that day when you welcome us in the house of the LORD. Amen

Fifth Sunday of Easter

S	Acts 11:1-18		Ps. 148
	Rev. 21:1-6		John 13:31-35
M	Lev. 19:9-18	**T**	Lev. 11:1-12, 41-47
W	Luke 10:25-28	**Th**	Ezek. 22:23-31
F	Rev. 10:1-11	**S**	Ps. 119:9-16

FOR PRAYER THROUGHOUT THE DAY

O God, save our household!
See *Acts 11:14*

A PRAYER FOR THE WEEK

Your Son asks us to do only one thing:
love one another.
Write his commandment in our hearts, O God,
and teach us to love in word and deed. Amen

Sixth Sunday of Easter

S	Acts 16:9-15		Ps. 67
	Rev. 21:10, 22-22:5		John 14:23-29
M	I Chron. 12:16-22	**T**	I Chron. 15:1-5
W	Luke 2:26-38		
Asc	Acts 1:1-11		Ps. 47
	Eph. 1:15-23		Luke 24:44-53
F	Rev 12:13-17	**S**	Ps 119:105-112

FOR PRAYER THROUGHOUT THE DAY

Lord, come and stay in our home.
See *Acts 16:15*

A PRAYER FOR THE WEEK

Great and Holy Spirit,
when we are fearful, give us courage;
when we are troubled, give us peace;
when we are cold, warm us with your love. Amen

Seventh Sunday of Easter

S	Acts 16:16-34		Ps. 97
	Rev. 22:12-14, 16-17, 20-21		John 17:20-26
M	Exod. 41:16-20	**T**	2 Chron. 5:2-14
W	Luke 9:18-27	**Th**	Num. 14:13-24
F	Rev. 19:9-21	**S**	Ps. 87

FOR PRAYER THROUGHOUT THE DAY

Come, Lord Jesus.
Revelation 22:20

A PRAYER FOR THE WEEK

Lord Jesus,
heal the wounds that divide your church,
and make us witnesses to the unity you desire
for the whole world. Amen

Pentecost

S	Acts 2:1-21		Ps. 104:24-34, 35b
	Rom. 8:14-17		John 14:8-17 [25-27]
M	Joel 2:18-29	**T**	Ezek. 11:14-25
W	John 20:19-23	**Th**	Num. 24:1-13
F	1 Cor. 2:1-13	**S**	Ps. 104

FOR PRAYER THROUGHOUT THE DAY

In wisdom you have made all things.
Psalm 104:24

A PRAYER FOR THE WEEK

Pour your Spirit upon us, O God,
so that we may dream dreams and
speak your life-giving word in daily life. Amen

Summer

*I*n the weeks after Pentecost we explore what it means to live in the eternal day that is ours through baptism into Christ's deathless life. In the weeks after Pentecost we explore what it means *to be:* to be children of God, to be in Christ, to be on fire with the Spirit. In the Northern Hemisphere we are in the midst of summer: we are no longer eagerly anticipating the sprouting of the seed to green; we are surrounded here by the lush green of the present. Not yet do we expect the dying of the year; for now, the green is with us. It is a bountiful time of being. It is a time of *isness,* as the Christian medieval mystic Meister Eckhart would say. Like the year, we too are allowed *to be* during these days. To be here. In this moment.

While the experience of the first half of the church's year of grace has been intensely an experience of becoming with Christ, the green season after Pentecost is a time to be aware of just who we have become. The opening festival of this season directs us to remember how we have come to this place, who has guided us, who fills us, who is our being: God revealed to us in the persons of the Holy Trinity. On this festival Wisdom calls us from the ordinary places—the roadside, the crossroads where we have been traveling—and cries out the wonder of God, creator of all from the beginning, whose love has been poured into our hearts by the Spirit of Christ. This is who we have become: people whose hearts are filled with God's burning love. How then, do we live as such people? How are the ordinary lives we lead shaped by this being?

For many Christians, these weeks are called Ordinary Time, "ordinary" meaning in regular rows or ranks undistinguished from one another. Day after day of ordinary days, week after week of ordinary weeks undistinguished from one another, unbroken by major festivals or feasts. Just like life. Day after day of being in ordinary places: home, school, work. This is the character of ordinary time—the days after Pentecost, the largest part of the church year, and of most of life—not a time of celebration, that draws us into wonder, not a time of crisis, that draws us into change, but ordinary time, a time of being.

Just what characterizes a life of being with God and people of God is seen in the biblical readings that surround and embrace us in these days, especially the gospel stories and parables. We meet Jesus as a person keenly alive, in tune with his surroundings, aware of people, feelings, sensations—he saw, he felt, he heard, he sensed. We meet Jesus as a person who, because he feels on his skin the tears of the woman with the jar of ointment, can forgive; who, because he hears the voice of the man tormented by demons, can release; who, because he is aware and present and sees the woman crippled for eighteen years, can heal.

To be is to be aware, and to be aware is to be fully present in the moment; to be present is to value and notice the messages of our senses which pull us into the present. This is why in worship all the senses are engaged—we see the worship space and the cross; we hear the music of praise and the biblical readings; we touch the hand of a neighbor and trace the cross on our body; we smell the incense and the flowers; we taste the wheat and the grape. And thus we are pulled out of the meandering mind of worry into Here; pulled out of the clinging mind of regret into Now. For it is only here where we are that we can be God's people, to heal and to bless. For it is only now that we can be Christ's body of love, to forgive and release.

God's love has been poured into our hearts, and, according to the season's scripture readings, the ordinary lives lived out of that love will be lives of forgiveness, courage, endurance, mercy, hospitality, prayer, humility, renunciation, trust.

When we live lives intensely aware, in tune with the present, filled with God's love toward all around us, our lives take on the vibrant green of the season, of ordinary life deeply alive.

Praying in Summer

INVITATION

Every generous act of giving, with every perfect gift,
is from above, coming down from the Father of lights.
James 1:17

TABLE PRAYER

With the sun, moon, and stars,
with the deep sea, hills, and trees,
with all creeping things and flying birds,
we give you praise, O Lord our creator.
We offer you thanks for the gifts of this table,
signs of your love and mercy.
We bless you for your Son,
who is our life, health, and salvation,
our food and drink, now and forever. Amen

HYMN

Many and great, O God, are your works,
maker of earth and sky.
Your hands have set the heav'ns with stars;
your fingers spread the hills and plains.
Lo, your word formed the waters deep;
oceans obey your voice.

Grant unto us communion with you,
O Star-abiding One.
Come unto us and dwell with us;
with you are found the gifts of life.
Bless us with life that has no end,
eternal life with you.
Tune: LAC QUI PARLE

PSALM 1:1-3

> Happy are those
>> who do not follow the advice of the wicked,
> or take the path that sinners tread,
>> or sit in the seat of scoffers;
> but their delight is in the law of the LORD,
>> and on his law they meditate day and night.
> They are like trees
>> planted by streams of water,
> which yield their fruit in its season,
>> and their leaves do not wither.
> In all that they do, they prosper.

SCRIPTURE

See the daily readings

CANTICLE

In the morning, the Song of Zechariah (page 21)
In the evening, the Song of Mary (page 26)
At bedtime, the Song of Simeon (page 29) or

> Blessed are those who trust in the LORD,
> whose trust is the LORD.
> They shall be like a tree planted by water,
> sending out its roots by the stream.

> It shall not fear when heat comes,
> and its leaves shall stay green;
> in the year of drought it is not anxious,
> and it does not cease to bear good fruit.
>> *Jeremiah 17:7-8*

PRAYER

Prayers for others and ourselves
The Lord's Prayer

God Most High,
by your Word you created a wondrous universe,
and through your Spirit you breathed into it the breath of life.
Accept creation's hymn of praise from our lips,
and let the praise that is sung in heaven
resound in the heart of every creature on earth,
to your glory, Father, Son, and Holy Spirit,
now and forever. Amen

Lord God,
you have called your servants to ventures
of which we cannot see the ending,
by paths as yet untrodden, through perils unknown.
Give us faith to go out with good courage,
not knowing where we go,
but only that your hand is leading us
and your love supporting us;
through Jesus Christ our Lord. Amen

BLESSING FOR TRAVELERS

Use this prayer before leaving on a journey

O God,
our beginning and our end,
you kept Abraham and Sarah in safety
throughout the days of their pilgrimage,
you led the children of Israel through the midst of the sea,
and by a star you led the Magi to the infant Jesus.
Protect and guide us now as we set out to travel.
Make our ways safe and our homecomings joyful,
and bring us at last to our heavenly home,
where you dwell in glory with our Lord Jesus Christ
and the life-giving Holy Spirit,
one God, now and forever. Amen

BLESSING FOR FATHER'S DAY

Use this prayer on the third Sunday in June

As a loving father cares for his children,
so you, O God, have compassion for us.
Look with favor on all those men
who guide and protect their children.
Hold them in your good care
and strengthen them for the holy task
which you have entrusted to them,
that all your children may flourish
in an atmosphere of wise love. Amen

A PRAYER FOR THOSE WHO LABOR IN THE FIELDS

Use this prayer whenever it is appropriate

Almighty God
we thank you for making the fruitful earth
produce what is needed for life.
Bless those who work in the fields;
give us favorable weather;
and grant that we may all share the fruits of the earth,
rejoicing in your goodness;
through your Son, Jesus our Lord. Amen

THANKSGIVING FOR EARTH'S PRODUCE

Use this prayer whenever appropriate in your home

Blessed are you, O Lord our God, creator of the universe,
for you bring forth food from the earth.
Blessed are you, O Lord our God, creator of the universe,
for you cause the grape and the grain to grow.
Blessed are you, O Lord our God, creator of the universe,
for from your lavish grace we are fed and nourished.
Exalted and glorified are you, O God,
exalted above all things,
for in your wisdom you create and sustain the earth
and all living creatures. Amen

Daily readings and prayers

Trinity Sunday

S Prov. 8:1-4, 22-31   Ps. 8
      Rom. 5:1-5   John 16:12-15
M Prov. 1:20—2:15   **T** Prov. 3:13-20
W Luke 1:67-79   **Th** Prov. 4:1-9
F Eph. 4:1-16   **S** Ps. 124

FOR PRAYER THROUGHOUT THE DAY

Hope does not disappoint us.
Romans 5:5

A PRAYER FOR THE WEEK

O Sacred Three,
fill us with your wisdom, mercy, and fire.
Pour your love into our hearts
and fill us with hope. Amen

Sunday between May 29 and June 4 (Proper 4)

S 1 Kings 8:22-23, 41-43   Ps. 96:1-9
      Gal. 1:1-12   Luke 7:1-10
M Ruth 1:1-18   **T** Ruth 4:7-22
W Luke 4:31-37   **Th** Jonah 4:1-11
F Acts 3:1-10   **S** Ps. 100

FOR PRAYER THROUGHOUT THE DAY

Keep me in your steadfast love.
See 1 Kings 8:23

A PRAYER FOR THE WEEK

Lord,
we are not worthy to receive you,
but only say the word and we shall be healed. Amen

Sunday between June 5 and 11 (Proper 5)

S	I Kings 17:17-24		Ps. 30
	Gal. 1:11-24		Luke 7:11-17
M	Gen. 22:1-14	**T**	Judg. 11:29-40
W	Luke 8:40-56	**Th**	Ezek. 37:1-14
F	Gal. 2:1-14	**S**	Ps. 28

FOR PRAYER THROUGHOUT THE DAY

O Lord, be my helper.
Psalm 30:10

A PRAYER FOR THE WEEK

O God,
open our eyes to see those who suffer
and train our hearts to ease their pain
for the sake of Christ our Lord. Amen

Sunday between June 12 and 18 (Proper 6)

S	2 Sam. 11:26—12:10, 13-15		Ps. 32
	Gal. 2:15-21		Luke 7:36—8:3
M	2 Chron. 30:1-12	**T**	2 Chron. 30:13-27
W	Luke 5:17-26	**Th**	Prov. 3:21-35
F	Gal. 3:1-14	**S**	Ps. 130

FOR PRAYER THROUGHOUT THE DAY

Christ lives in me.
Galatians 2:20

A PRAYER FOR THE WEEK

Merciful God,
open our hearts to receive your forgiveness
and grant us your peace. Amen

Sunday between June 19 and 25 (Proper 7)

S Isa. 65:1-9   Ps. 22:19-28
   Gal. 3:23-29   Luke 8:26-39
M Job 18:1-21   **T** Job 19:1-22
W Luke 9:37-43   **Th** Ezek. 32:1-10
F Gal. 3:15-22   **S** Ps. 6

FOR PRAYER THROUGHOUT THE DAY

O LORD, do not be far away from me.
Psalm 22:19

A PRAYER FOR THE WEEK

O God,
in baptism you have clothed us with Christ.
Forgive us when we fail to act in charity
toward our brothers and sisters. Amen

Sunday between June 26 and July 2 (Proper 8)

S I Kings 19:15-16, 19-21   Ps. 16
   Gal. 5:1, 13-25   Luke 9:51-62
M Gen. 19:15-29   **T** 2 Kings 1:9-16
W Luke 9:21-27   **Th** Lev. 9:22—10:11
F Gal. 4:8-19   **S** Ps. 140

FOR PRAYER THROUGHOUT THE DAY

Show me the path of life.
Psalm 16:11

A PRAYER FOR THE WEEK

Holy Spirit,
nourish your gifts within me.
Teach me to be peaceful, patient, and generous. Amen

Sunday between July 3 and 9 (Proper 9)

S Isa. 66:10-14 Ps. 66:1-9
Gal. 6:[1-6] 7-16 Luke 10:1-11, 16-20
M Jer. 6:10-19 **T** Jer. 8:4-12
W Luke 9:1-6 **Th** Josh. 23:1-16
F Gal. 4:50—5:1 **S** Ps. 125

FOR PRAYER THROUGHOUT THE DAY

Mothering God, hold us in your strong arms
See *Isaiah 66:12-13*

A PRAYER FOR THE WEEK

Make it our one desire, O God,
to love you with heart, soul, and mind,
and to confirm that love with our service to those in need. Amen

Sunday between July 10 and 16 (Proper 10)

S Deut. 30:9-14 Ps. 25:1-10
Col. 1:1-14 Luke 10:25-37
M Gen. 41:14-36 **T** Gen. 41:37-49
W John 3:16-21 **Th** Lev. 19:1-4, 32-37
F James 2:14-26 **S** Ps. 25

FOR PRAYER THROUGHOUT THE DAY

O God, in you I trust.
Psalm 25:1

A PRAYER FOR THE WEEK

Let the gospel of love grow within us,
O God our creator.
Make us strong and help us to endure everything
with patience as we wait for the return of your Son. Amen

Sunday between July 17 and 23 (Proper 11)

S Gen. 18:1-10a   Ps. 15
      Col. 1:15-28   Luke 10:38-42
M Exod. 18:1-12   **T** 2 Chron. 29:10-23
W Luke 8:4-8   **Th** Deut. 12:1-7
F Col. 1:27—2:7   **S** Ps. 145

FOR PRAYER THROUGHOUT THE DAY

LORD, lead me to your holy hill.
See Psalm 15:1

A PRAYER FOR THE WEEK

Lord Jesus,
draw us into your life
and fill us with the mystery of your wisdom. Amen

Sunday between July 24 and 30 (Proper 12)

S Gen. 18:20-32   Ps. 138
      Col. 2:6-15 [16-19]   Luke 11:1-13
M Esther 3:7-15   **T** Esther 7:1-10
W Luke 8:22-25   **Th** Job 22:21—23:27
F Col. 2:20—3:1   **S** Ps. 39

FOR PRAYER THROUGHOUT THE DAY

Your kingdom come.
Luke 11:2

A PRAYER FOR THE WEEK

Creator of all that is good,
keep our hearts open
so that when our neighbor calls in need,
we may respond with generosity.
Hear us for the sake of him
so that we might become rich. Amen

Sunday between July 31 and Aug. 6 (Proper 13)

S   Eccles. 1:2, 12-13; 2:18-23   Ps. 49:1-12
      Col. 3:1-11   Luke 12:13-21
M   Eccles. 2:1-17   **T**   Eccles. 3:16—4:8
W   Luke 12:22-31   **Th** Eccles. 12:1-8, 13-14
F   Col. 3:18—4:5   **S**   Ps. 40

FOR PRAYER THROUGHOUT THE DAY

I have been raised with Christ.
> See *Colossians 3:1*

A PRAYER FOR THE WEEK

What will endure beyond the grave, O God?
Teach us to hold fast to the riches of your kingdom
and to cherish the life you have given us in baptism. Amen

Sunday between Aug. 7 and 13 (Proper 14)

S   Gen. 15:1-6   Ps. 33:12-22
      Heb. 11:1-3, 8-16   Luke 12:32-40
M   Gen. 17:9-27   **T**   2 Chron. 34:22-33
W   Luke 12:41-48   **Th** Jer. 33:14-26
F   Heb. 11:1-7, 17-28   **S**   Ps. 89:1-18

FOR PRAYER THROUGHOUT THE DAY

Jesus says, do not be afraid.
> *Luke 12:32*

A PRAYER FOR THE WEEK

Gracious God,
ready our hearts for your coming.
As we celebrate your banquet here,
let our eyes stay fixed on unfailing treasure in heaven. Amen

Sunday between Aug. 14 and 20 (Proper 15)

S   Jer. 23:23-29   Ps. 82
      Heb. 11:29—12:2   Luke 12:49-56
M   I Sam. 5:1-12   **T**   I Sam. 6:10-16
W   Luke 19:45-48   **Th**   Josh. 7:1, 10-26
F   Heb. 10:26-39   **S**   Ps. 39

FOR PRAYER THROUGHOUT THE DAY

Rescue the weak and the needy.
Psalm 82:4

A PRAYER FOR THE WEEK

God ever-near,
give us wisdom to interpret the signs of our time
so that we might know how to serve your gospel. Amen

Sunday between Aug. 21 and 27 (Proper 16)

S   Isa. 58:9b-14   Ps. 103:1-8
      Heb. 12:18-29   Luke 13:10-17
M   Exod. 31:12-17   **T**   Isa. 56:1-5
W   Luke 14:1-6   **Th**   Acts 13:13-16, 26-43
F   Heb. 12:1-17   **S**   Ps. 103

FOR PRAYER THROUGHOUT THE DAY

Free us, Jesus, from our burdens.
See *Luke 13:12*

A PRAYER FOR THE WEEK

Gracious God,
you ask us to feed the hungry
and to relieve the suffering of the afflicted.
Give us strength to do your will
for the sake of Christ our Lord. Amen

Autumn

See, I have set before you today life and prosperity, death and adversity. . . .
Choose life so that you and your descendants may live, loving the LORD *your*
God, obeying him, and holding fast to him, for that means life to you.
Deuteronomy 30:15, 20

While Christians celebrate this season with the color
green, many people in our land are beginning to see
gold, orange, and scarlet in the natural world. The year is
maturing, and the gold reminds us of harvest, the orange, of
bounty, and the scarlet, of change. We are still exploring what
it means to be, to be a people alive with the presence of God.
But with this bright and glory-filled show of color in the natural world, we sense with wonder that the end of the year is
coming, and our thoughts, like the leaves, turn.

The season of autumn, as it comes in contact with the
days after Pentecost, draws our attention to thoughts of harvest. Harvest festivals abound during this time: Lammastide,
the first wheat harvest; Lugnasad, the Celtic beginning of
harvest; Sukkoth, originally the Jewish celebration of the first
wine harvest; Thanksgiving, a harvest festival.

But the changing of the year brings with it an awareness
of another harvest, a harvest associated with the ending of all
days: a harvest of deeds and of lives. It is a time to reconsider,
to reassess, to refocus the intent of our lives, to realize where
we have lost sight of the truth. At this time of the year, many
of the biblical readings seem hard and unyielding. No matter
how complacently we may live in the belief that we are saved
by God's grace, the voice of scripture in these days makes it

uncompromisingly clear that God expects our faith to bear fruit. God says to us, "What will you choose, life or death?" What will be harvested from this life we are living?

At this time of year, at Rosh Hashanah, the Jewish people hear the sound of the ram's horn, the *shofar*, calling them to examine their lives, to change their ways. The Jewish scholar Maimonides wrote that the shofar calls to the people: "Awake you sleepers, from your sleep! Rouse yourselves, you slumberers, out of your slumber! Examine your deeds, and turn to God in repentance. Remember your Creator, you who are caught up in the daily round, losing sight of the truth."

Remember the Creator—who sets before us life and death, and urges us to choose life. The words of Luke's Gospel and the readings from Paul's letters are no less uncompromising: "Whoever does not carry the cross and follow me cannot be my disciple" (Luke 14:26); "You cannot serve God and wealth" (Luke 16:13); "We brought nothing into the world, so that we can take nothing out of it" (1 Tim. 6:6); "All who exalt themselves will be humbled . . ." (Luke 18:14).

We cannot escape these pronouncements, and we delude ourselves if we try to avoid their implications for our ordinary lives. God asks, "Which will you choose: life or death?" God further declares that the way of life is to love God, obey God, and hold fast to God. Where in our lives do we not love God? Where in our lives do we not obey God? Where in our lives do we not hold fast to God?

This time of year asks of us that we set priorities—priorities for the use of our days, for the use of our talents, for the use of our wealth; priorities for our love, our loyalty, our obedience; priorities as to who or what will be our God.

Paul, writing to Timothy, says to "pursue righteousness, godliness, faith, love, endurance, gentleness." These qualities simply stand in contrast to many of the enticements of our age: possessiveness, wealth, expediency, influence, power over others. What guides our choices? The biblical readings ask: Who is our God? What governs the ultimate choices of our existence? Have we lost sight of eternal truth?

In wrestling with these hard questions we are much like Jacob wrestling with God, and, like Jacob, who walked away from the encounter with a limp, we may never walk exactly the same way again.

All around us the harvest is being brought in; all around us the autumn days are asking: What will be the harvest from this life we are living? Whether we live the lives of gardeners or bankers or students or bakers or parents or engineers, what will the harvest be?

Praying in Autumn

INVITATION

See, I have set before you today life and prosperity,
death and adversity.
Choose life so that you and your descendants may live.
Deuteronomy 3:15, 19

TABLE PRAYER

The eyes of all wait upon you, O Lord,
and you give them their food in due season.
We praise you, O God, for autumn days
and for the gifts of this table.
Grant us grace to share your goodness
until all people are fed by the harvest of the earth,
through Christ our Lord. Amen

HYMN

Praise and thanksgiving, God we would offer
for all things living you have made good;
harvest of sown fields, fruits of the orchard,
hay from the mown fields, blossom and wood.

You are providing food for your children,
your wisdom guiding teaches us share
one with another, so that, rejoicing
with us, all others may know your care.

Then will your blessing reach every people,
all earth confessing your gracious hand.
Where you are reigning no one will hunger,
your love sustaining fruitful the land.
Tune: BUNESSAN

PSALM 37:1-9

Do not fret because of the wicked;
   do not be envious of wrongdoers,
for they will soon fade like the grass,
   and wither like the green herb.

Trust in the LORD, and do good;
     so you will live in the land, and enjoy security.
Take delight in the LORD,
     and he will give you the desires of your heart.

Commit your way to the LORD;
     trust in him, and he will act.

He will make your vindication shine like the light,
     and the justice of your cause like the noonday.

Be still before the LORD, and wait patiently for him;
     do not fret over those who prosper in their way,
     over those who carry out evil devices.
Refrain from anger, and forsake wrath.
     Do not fret—it leads only to evil.
For the wicked shall be cut off,
     but those who wait for the LORD shall inherit the land.

SCRIPTURE

See the daily readings

CANTICLE

In the morning, the Song of Zechariah (page 21)
In the evening, the Song of Mary (page 26)
At bedtime, the Song of Simeon (page 29) or

Keep in mind that Jesus Christ has died for us
and is risen from the dead.
He is our saving Lord; he is joy for all ages.

If we die with the Lord, we shall live with the Lord.
If we endure with the Lord, we shall live with the Lord.

In him all our sorrow, in him all our joy.
In him hope of glory, in him all our love.

In him our redemption, in him all our grace.
In him our salvation, in him all our peace.
          See *2 Timothy 2:8, 11-13*

PRAYER

Prayers for others and ourselves
The Lord's Prayer

O gracious Father,
when you open your hand you satisfy the desire of every living
    thing.
Bless the land and waters, and give the world a plentiful harvest.
As you show your love and kindness in the bounty of the land
    and sea,
save us from the selfish use of your gifts,
so that men and women everywhere may give you thanks,
through Jesus Christ our Lord. Amen

Direct us, O Lord, in all our doings
with your most gracious favor
and guide us with your continual help.
In all our works begun, continued, and ended in you,
may we glorify your holy name
and finally, by your mercy, obtain everlasting life,
through Jesus Christ our Lord. Amen

Teach us to number our days, O Lord,
that we may gain wisdom. Amen
    See *Psalm 90:12*

BLESSING FOR THE SCHOOL YEAR

Use this prayer before the beginning of school or study

All-knowing God,
you have created us with a desire for truth
and set before us the mysteries of your universe.
In our time of study,
give us curious minds and the delight of discovery,
that our whole lives may be a journey
into the knowledge of you
and the revelation of your will. Amen

BLESSING FOR STUDENTS AND TEACHERS

Use this prayer at the beginning of the school year or whenever appropriate

For the marvels of your creation, we praise you, O God.
For the opportunity to explore and study, we praise you, O God.
For those who guide us, teachers and mentors, we praise you,
    O God.
Teach us your ways and guide us in your path,
for you are the creator of all that is seen and unseen. Amen

SAINT LUKE, EVANGELIST

Use this prayer on St. Luke's Day, October 18

Almighty God,
you inspired your servant Luke the physician
to reveal in his gospel the love and healing power of your Son.
Give your church the same love and power to heal
to the glory of your name,
through your Son, Jesus Christ our Lord,
who lives and reigns with you and the Holy Spirit,
one God, now and forever. Amen

Daily readings and prayers

Sunday between Aug. 28 and Sept. 3 (Proper 17)

S	Prov. 25:6-7		Ps. 112
	Heb. 13:1-8, 15-16		Luke 14:1, 7-14
M	2 Chron. 12:1-12	**T**	2 Chron. 33:1-17
W	Luke 14:15-24	**Th**	Isa. 57:14-21
F	Heb. 13:7-21	**S**	Ps. 119:65-80

FOR PRAYER THROUGHOUT THE DAY

Lord Jesus, speak your word to me.
See *Hebrews 13:7*

A PRAYER FOR THE WEEK

Lord Jesus,
you invite all people to your banquet table:
the poor, the crippled, the lame, and the blind.
Teach us to follow your example
and to welcome all people in your name. Amen

Sunday between Sept. 4 and 10 (Proper 18)

S	Deut. 30:15-20		Ps. 1
	Philemon 1-21		Luke 14:25-33
M	Deut. 29:2-29	**T**	2 Kings 17:24-41
W	Luke 18:18-30	**Th**	Deut. 7:12-26
F	1 Tim. 3:11—4:16	**S**	Ps. 119:161-179

FOR PRAYER THROUGHOUT THE DAY

Help me choose life, that I might live.
See *Deuteronomy 30:19*

A PRAYER FOR THE WEEK

Lord Jesus,
open our hands and free us from anything
that prevents us from embracing you. Amen

Sunday between Sept. 11 and 17 (Proper 19)

S	Exod. 32:7-14		Ps. 51:1-10
	I Tim. 1:12-17		Luke 15:1-10
M	Amos 7:1-6	**T**	Jonah 3:1-10
W	Luke 22:54-62	**Th**	Job 40:6-14; 42:1-6
F	I Tim. 1:1-11	**S**	Ps. 51

FOR PRAYER THROUGHOUT THE DAY

Have mercy on me, O God.
Psalm 51:1

A PRAYER FOR THE WEEK

Create in me a clean heart, O God,
and put a new and right spirit within me.
Restore to me the joy of your salvation,
and sustain in me a willing spirit. Amen
Psalm 51:10, 12

Sunday between Sept. 18 and 24 (Proper 20)

S	Amos 8:4-7		Ps. 113
	I Tim. 2:1-7		Luke 16:1-13
M	Prov. 14:12-31	**T**	Prov. 17:1-5
W	Luke 20:45—21:4	**Th**	Ezek. 16:43-52
F	I Tim. 3:1-13	**S**	Ps. 10

FOR PRAYER THROUGHOUT THE DAY

You cannot serve God and wealth.
Luke 16:13

A PRAYER FOR THE WEEK

Lord Jesus,
help us to be faithful with the gifts
your Spirit has given us.
You ask no more than our trust in your goodwill
and willing hearts eager to serve those in need. Amen

Sunday between Sept. 25 and Oct. 1 (Proper 21)

S	Amos 6:1a, 4-7		Ps. 146
	I Tim. 6:6-19		Luke 16:19-31
M	Prov. 22:2-16	**T**	Prov 28:3-10
W	Luke 9:46-48	**Th**	Ezek. 18:5-24
F	Rev. 3:14-22	**S**	Ps. 9

FOR PRAYER THROUGHOUT THE DAY

I will praise you LORD as long as I live.
See *Psalm 146:2*

A PRAYER FOR THE WEEK

God our provider,
teach us to share what you have given us
with each other and those in need.
Open our eyes to see Christ
in all who suffer. Amen

Sunday between Oct. 2 and 8 (Proper 22)

S	Hab. 1:1-4; 2:1-4		Ps. 37:1-9
	2 Tim. 1:1-14		Luke 17:5-10
M	2 Kings 18:1-8, 8-36	**T**	2 Kings 19:8-20, 35-37
W	Luke 5:12-16	**Th**	Isa. 7:1-9
F	Rev. 2:12-29	**S**	Ps. 56

FOR PRAYER THROUGHOUT THE DAY

Increase our faith.
Luke 17:5

A PRAYER FOR THE WEEK

God of grace and mercy,
enkindle within us your Spirit
and help us use the good treasure of the gospel. Amen

Sunday between Oct. 9 and 15 (Proper 23)

S 2 Kings 5:1-3, 7-15c   Ps. 111
      2 Tim. 2:8-15   Luke 17:11-19
M Num. 12:1-15   **T** Lev. 14:33-53
W Luke 18:35-43   **Th** Neh. 13:1-3, 23-30
F 2 Tim. 2:1-7   **S** Ps. 41

FOR PRAYER THROUGHOUT THE DAY

Jesus, have mercy on us.
Luke 17:13

A PRAYER FOR THE WEEK

Merciful Savior,
you heal those who cry out to you.
Free us from anything that would prevent us
from knowing your love. Amen

Sunday between Oct. 16 and 22 (Proper 24)

S Gen. 32:22-31   Ps. 121
      2 Tim. 3:14—4:5   Luke 18:1-8
M I Sam. 25:1-22   **T** I Sam. 25:23-42
W Luke 22:39-46   **Th** Isa. 54:11-17
F 2 Tim. 2:14-26   **S** Ps. 57

FOR PRAYER THROUGHOUT THE DAY

My help comes from the Lord, who made heaven and earth.
Psalm 121:2

A PRAYER FOR THE WEEK

Just and merciful God,
you hear the cries of your people.
Grant us the courage to pray always and never lose heart. Amen

Sunday between Oct. 23 and 29 (Proper 25)

S Jer. 14:7-10, 19-22   Ps. 84:1-7
   2 Tim. 4:6-8, 16-18   Luke 18:9-14
M Dan. 5:1-12   **T** Dan. 5:13-31
W Luke 1:46-55   **Th** 1 Sam. 2:1-10
F 2 Tim. 3:1-15   **S** Ps. 84

FOR PRAYER THROUGHOUT THE DAY

O God, we set our hope on you.
Jeremiah 14:22

A PRAYER FOR THE WEEK

Loving God,
be merciful to me, a sinner. Amen
Luke 18:13

November

In the blessedness of your saints you have given us a glorious pledge of the hope of our calling; that moved by their witness and supported by their fellowship, we may run with perseverence the race that is set before us and with them receive the unfading crown of glory. Preface for All Saints

Humans are, by nature, creatures who not only work and think, but who sing, dance, pray, celebrate, and tell stories. The stories we tell as people of God ground us in a great unfolding of creation of which we are neither the beginning nor the ending. Our stories give us roots in an ongoing community, broadening our vision and our sense of purpose and place. The stories we recount at this time of the year, at the dying of the year, are especially stories of remembrance and stories of hope.

At the fading of the year, we may be drawn to contemplate the fading of life—our own lives, those of family members, our ancestors, or the saints. By calling to remembrance those who have died, we connect ourselves to previous generations and take our place in the passing on of knowledge and wisdom. Without the stories of our ancestors we must learn everything by ourselves; we must lose our way and struggle and search, perhaps vainly. Without the wisdom of our ancestors, we are like those suffering with amnesia who have forgotten who they are. The memory of our ancestors in faith, which we call to mind at this fading of the year, weaves us into a story that we do not need to begin on our own, but only to continue.

We sing the wisdom of our ancestors in the psalms and the hymns they wrote; we pray with them in the ancient liturgies distilled over hundreds of years from myriad encounters with the Holy One. We listen to their stories as the Bible is read, as we read the lives of the saints, as we share memories at a funeral. And as we worship and sing, as we kneel and give thanks, they surround us and join us. "Therefore with angels and archangels and all the company of heaven we praise your name and join their *unending hymn*" (emphasis added). It should take our breath away to consider all the company of heaven joining us in praising God who fills both heaven and earth with glory.

So at the dying of the year, there are the festivals for calling to mind those who have died—All Saints, All Souls. We light candles. We visit graves. We pray in thanks. We sing *requiem*. And also, at the dying of the year, there is a festival to celebrate the hope that binds us all: Christ the King, or the Sunday of Fulfillment, or, simply, the Last Sunday.

"I will gather the remnant of my flock . . . they shall not fear any longer, or be dismayed," God declares through the prophet Jeremiah. Hope can shape our lives by eradicating fear now. Remembrance will shape our lives by showing us the reason we dare hope. Thus the past and the future are brought together to form and inform our present lives, connecting us to the origin of our hope and to the destiny of our remembrance. "Be glad and rejoice forever in what I am creating," says the Lord.

We all know intuitively that the dying of the year is not the end. We see in each circle of the year the light of spring emerge from winter's darkness. This God also declares to us, that the end of our lives is not the end, that the end of the present time is not the end forever, that newness is in the very fabric of creation, and God is the loving cause of it. "For I am about to create new heavens and a new earth, the former things shall not be remembered or come to mind. But be glad and rejoice forever in what I am creating." Amen

Praying in November

INVITATION

Blessed are the dead who, from now on, die in the Lord.
They will rest from their labors, for their deeds follow them.
Revelation 14:13

TABLE PRAYER

As we share this meal, eternal God,
we praise you for the gift of salvation
made known to us in Jesus Christ.
We offer you thanks
for those who have gone before us in faith.
Bring us with them to the great feast of heaven
where all your children will be welcome at your table.
Grant this through Christ our Lord
whose coming is certain and whose day draws near. Amen

HYMN

I want to walk as a child of the light.
I want to follow Jesus.
God set the stars to give light to the world.
The star of my life is Jesus.

In him there is no darkness at all.
The night and the day are both alike.
The Lamb is the light of the city of God.
Shine in my heart, Lord Jesus.

I want to see the brightness of God.
I want to look at Jesus.
Clear Sun of Righteousness, shine on my path,
and show me the way to the Father.
Refrain

I'm looking for the coming of Christ.
I want to be with Jesus.
When we have run with patience the race,
we shall know the joy of Jesus.
Refrain

> *Tune:* HOUSTON

PSALM 46:1-7, 10-11

God is our refuge and strength,
  a very present help in trouble.
Therefore we will not fear, though the earth should change,
  though the mountains shake in the heart of the sea;
though the waters roar and foam,
  though the mountains tremble with its tumult.

There is a river whose streams make glad the city of God,
  the holy habitation of the Most High.
God is in the midst of the city; it shall not be moved;
  God will help it when the morning dawns.
The nations are in an uproar, the kingdoms totter;
  he utters his voice, the earth melts.

"Be still and know that I am God!
  I am exalted among the nations,
  I am exalted in the earth."
The LORD of hosts is with us;
  the God of Jacob is our refuge.

SCRIPTURE

See the daily readings

CANTICLE

In the morning, the Song of Zechariah (page 21)
In the evening, the Song of Mary (page 26)
At bedtime, the Song of Simeon (page 29) or

Holy, holy, holy,
the Lord God the Almighty,
who was and is and is to come.
You are worthy, our Lord and God,
to receive glory and honor and power
for you created all things,
and by your will they existed and were created.

You are worthy to take the scroll
and to open its seals,
for you were slaughtered and by your blood
you ransomed for God
saints from every tribe and language and people and nation;
you have made them to be a kingdom and priests serving our God,
and they will reign on earth.

Worthy is the Lamb that was slaughtered
to receive power and wealth and wisdom and might
and honor and glory and blessing!

To the one seated on the throne
and to the Lamb
be blessing and honor and glory and might
forever and ever. Amen
Revelation 4:8, 11; 5:9-10, 12-14

PRAYER

Prayers for others and ourselves
The Lord's Prayer

God of all time, God of all space,
into the dying of the year
we call your faithful presence.
Into the fading of lives and of dreams
we summon your unfailing promises.
Strengthen us with the vision of your new Jerusalem.
Encourage us with the singing of the heavenly congregation.
Lead us on the path of justice and peace
to the holy city where you dwell,
Father, Son, and Holy Spirit,
now and forever. Amen

THANKSGIVING FOR THE FAITHFUL DEPARTED

Use this prayer in the home or at the grave

In peace let us pray to the Lord.
Lord, have mercy.
May God, Comfort of all,
who has blessed us with sisters and brothers,
companions on this journey,
guard and protect all who have departed
from this sphere of life,
that theirs may be a rest in the radiant presence of God. Amen

PRAYER FOR A PEACEFUL DEATH

In peace let us pray to the Lord.
Lord, have mercy.
May God, Creator of all,
who has given us the times and the seasons,
the dawning and the twilight of days and of lives,
fill us with quiet trust in all seasons of life,
that when death draws near to embrace us,
we may with a peaceful heart let go
into that mysterious sleep. Amen

PRAYER FOR THE LAST SUNDAY, CHRIST THE KING

God and Father of our Lord Jesus Christ,
you gave us your Son,
the beloved one who was rejected,
the Savior who appeared defeated.
Yet the mystery of his kingship illumines our lives.
Show us in his death the victory that crowns the ages,
and in his broken body
the love that unites heaven and earth.
We ask this through your Son, our Lord Jesus Christ,
who lives and reigns with you in the unity of the Holy Spirit,
one God, forever and ever. Amen

BLESSING FOR THANKSGIVING DAY

Use this prayer at a Thanksgiving meal or whenever appropriate

Blessing and honor to you, God of the harvest,
for the days and the seasons, the harvest of days;
for the fruits and grains, harvest of earth;
for wine and bread, harvest of handiwork;
for family and companions,
for forebears and saints,
for the rich abundance of your love
revealed in Christ, our true food and drink.
Blessing and honor to you, God of the harvest. Amen

Daily readings and prayers

All Saints Day

Dan. 7:1-3, 15-18   Ps. 149
Eph. 1:11-23   Luke 6:20-31

FOR PRAYER THROUGHOUT THE DAY

Make us living witnesses of your unchanging love.

Sunday between Oct. 30 and Nov. 5 (Proper 26)

S   Isa. 1:10-18   Ps. 32:1-7
        2 Thess. 1:1-4, 11-12   Luke 19:1-10
M   Amos 5:12-24   **T** Zech. 7:1-14
W   Luke 19:11-27   **Th** Prov. 15:8-11, 24-33
F   Jude 5-21   **S** Ps. 50

FOR PRAYER THROUGHOUT THE DAY

Lord, I will give to the poor.
Luke 19:8

A PRAYER FOR THE WEEK

Lord Jesus,
stay at our house this day.
Be present at our table
and feed us with your mercy. Amen

Sunday between Nov. 6 and 12 (Proper 27)

S	Job 19:23-27a		Ps. 17:1-9
	2 Thess. 2:1-5, 13-17		Luke 20:27-38
M	Deut. 25:5-10	T	Gen. 38:1-26
W	Luke 20:1-8	Th	Exod. 3:1-15
F	Acts 24:1-23	S	Ps. 17

FOR PRAYER THROUGHOUT THE DAY

Comfort our hearts and strengthen us in every good work.
2 Thessalonians 2:17

A PRAYER FOR THE WEEK

God of the living,
you have called us through your Spirit
to work in our troubled world.
Strengthen us in our ministry
as witnesses to the risen Lord. Amen

Sunday between Nov. 13 and 19 (Proper 28)

S	Mal. 4:1-2a		Ps. 98
	2 Thess. 3:6-13		Luke 21:5-19
M	2 Sam. 13:1-14	T	2 Sam. 13:23-46
W	Luke 17:20-37	Th	Ezek. 10:1-22
F	2 Thess. 1:3-12	S	Ps. 44

FOR PRAYER THROUGHOUT THE DAY

Lord, may we never grow weary in doing what is right.
See 2 Thessalonians 3:13

A PRAYER FOR THE WEEK

Lord Jesus,
keep us faithful to your word
and enlighten us with your wisdom
on the path of life. Amen

Christ the King (Proper 29)

S   Jer 23:1-6   Ps 46
       Col 1:11-20   Luke 23:33-43
M   Ps 24   **T**   Ps 48
W   Luke 18:15-17   **Th** Isa 33:17-22
F   Rev 21:5-27   **S**   John 21:24-25

FOR PRAYER THROUGHOUT THE DAY

Jesus, remember me when you come into your kingdom.
Luke 23:42

A PRAYER FOR THE WEEK

In your kingdom, Lord Jesus,
the poor are crowned with mercy
and the lowly rejoice in the triumph of justice.
Strengthen us to serve your reign of peace
until that day when all things are restored in you. Amen

Church year calendar for Year of Luke (Cycle C)

Day	1997-1998	2000-2001	2003-2004	2006-2007	2009-2010
First Sunday in Advent	Nov 30, 1997	Dec 3, 2000	Nov 30, 2003	Dec 3, 2006	Nov 29, 2009
Baptism of our Lord	Jan 11	Jan 7	Jan 11	Jan 7	Jan 10
Transfiguration of our Lord	Feb 22	Feb 25	Feb 22	Feb 18	Feb 1
Ash Wednesday	Feb 25	Feb 28	Feb 25	Feb 21	Feb 17
First Sunday in Lent	Mar 1	Mar 4	Feb 29	Feb 25	Feb 21
Passion Sunday	Apr 5	Apr 8	Apr 4	Apr 1	Mar 28
Maundy Thursday	Apr 9	Apr 12	Apr 8	Apr 5	Apr 1
Good Friday	Apr 10	Apr 13	Apr 9	Apr 6	Apr 2
Vigil of Easter	Apr 11	Apr 14	Apr 10	Apr 7	Apr 3
Resurrection of our Lord	Apr 12	Apr 15	Apr 11	Apr 8	Apr 4
Ascension of our Lord	May 21	May 24	May 20	May 17	May 13
Day of Pentecost	May 31	June 3	May 30	May 27	May 23
Trinity Sunday	June 7	June 10	June 6	June 3	May 30
S. btwn. June 5 and 11 (Pr. 5)				June 10	June 6
S. btwn. June 12 and 18 (Pr. 6)	June 14	June 17	June 13	June 17	June 13
S. btwn. June 19 and 25 (Pr. 7)	June 21	June 24	June 20	June 24	June 20
S. btwn. June 26 and July 2 (Pr. 8)	June 28	July 1	June 27	July 1	June 27
S. btwn. July 3 and 9 (Pr. 9)	July 5	July 8	July 4	July 8	July 4
S. btwn. July 10 and 16 (Pr. 10)	July 12	July 15	July 11	July 15	July 11
S. btwn. July 17 and 23 (Pr. 11)	July 19	July 22	July 18	July 22	July 18
S. btwn. July 24 and 30 (Pr. 12)	July 26	July 29	July 25	July 29	July 25

Day	1997-1998	2000-2001	2003-2004	2006-2007	2009-2010
S. btwn. July 31 and Aug 6 (Pr. 13)	Aug 2	Aug 5	Aug 1	Aug 5	Aug 1
S. btwn. Aug 7 and 13 (Pr. 14)	Aug 9	Aug 12	Aug 8	Aug 12	Aug 8
S. btwn. Aug 14 and 20 (Pr. 15)	Aug 16	Aug 19	Aug 15	Aug 19	Aug 15
S. btwn. Aug 21 and 27 (Pr. 16)	Aug 23	Aug 26	Aug 22	Aug 26	Aug 22
S. btwn. Aug 28 and Sept 3 (Pr. 17)	Aug 30	Sept 2	Aug 29	Sept 2	Aug 29
S. btwn. Sept 4 and 10 (Pr. 18)	Sept 6	Sept 9	Sept 5	Sept 9	Sept 5
S. btwn. Sept 11 and 17 (Pr. 19)	Sept 13	Sept 16	Sept 12	Sept 16	Sept 12
S. btwn. Sept 18 and 24 (Pr. 20)	Sept 20	Sept 23	Sept 19	Sept 23	Sept 19
S. btwn. Sept 25 and Oct 1 (Pr. 21)	Sept 27	Sept 30	Sept 26	Sept 30	Sept 26
S. btwn. Oct. 2 and 8 (Pr. 22)	Oct 4	Oct 7	Oct 3	Oct 7	Oct 3
S. btwn. Oct 9 and 15 (Pr. 23)	Oct 11	Oct 14	Oct 10	Oct 14	Oct 10
S. btwn. Oct 16 and 22 (Pr. 24)	Oct 18	Oct 21	Oct 17	Oct 21	Oct 17
S. btwn. Oct 23 and 29 (Pr. 25)	Oct 25	Oct 28	Oct 24	Oct 28	Oct 24
S. btwn. Oct 30 and Nov 5 (Pr. 26)	Nov 1	Nov 4	Oct 31	Nov 4	Oct 31
S. btwn. Nov 6 and 12 (Pr. 27)	Nov 8	Nov 11	Nov 7	Nov 11	Nov 7
S. btwn. Nov 13 and 19 (Pr. 28)	Nov 15	Nov 18	Nov 14	Nov 18	Nov 14
Christ the King	Nov 22	Nov 25	Nov 21	Nov 25	Nov 21
Day of Thanksgiving—Canada	Oct 12	Oct 8	Oct 11	Oct 8	Oct 11
Day of Thanksgiving—U.S.A.	Nov 26	Nov 22	Nov 25	Nov 29	Nov 25

Hymn Index

LBW refers to *Lutheran Book of Worship*; *WOV* refers to *With One Voice*. Many of these hymns are also found in other hymnals.

Daily Prayer

This day God gives me is sung to the tune BUNESSAN ("Morning has broken" or "Praise and thanksgiving, Father, we offer," LBW 409; "Baptized in water," WOV 693).

Christ, mighty Savior (INNISFREE FARM, WOV 729) may be sung to CHRISTE SANCTORUM ("Father, most holy," LBW 169).

All praise to you, my God this night (TALLIS' CANON, LBW 278) may be sung to OLD HUNDREDTH ("Praise God from whom all blessings flow," LBW 529).

God, who made the earth (LBW 281) is sung to the tune AR HYD Y NOS ("For the fruit of all creation," WOV 760; "Go, my children, with my blessing," WOV 721).

Sun of my soul (TALLIS' CANON) may be sung to OLD HUNDREDTH ("Praise God from whom all blessings flow," LBW 529).

Thy holy wings, O Savior (BRED DINA VIDA VINGAR, WOV 741) may be sung to AURELIA ("The church's one foundation," LBW 369) or MUNICH ("O Jesus, I have promised," LBW 503).

Sunday

Come, let us join our cheerful songs (NUN DANKET ALL, LBW 254) may be sung to ST. ANNE ("O God, our help in ages past," LBW 320) or LAND OF REST ("Jerusalem, my happy home," LBW 331).

O Trinity, O blessed light (O HEILIGE DREIFALTIGKEIT, LBW 275) may be sung to TALLIS' CANON ("All praise to thee, my God, this night," LBW 278) or DUKE STREET ("Jesus shall reign," LBW 530).

Advent

People, look east (BESANÇON) is at WOV 626.

Christmas

Angels we have heard on high (GLORIA) is at LBW 71.

Epiphany

Arise, your light has come! (FESTAL SONG, WOV 652) may be sung to SOUTH-WELL ("Lord Jesus, think on me," LBW 309) or DENNIS ("Blest be the tie that binds," LBW 370).

Lent

O Sun of justice, Jesus Christ (JESUS DULCIS MEMORIA, WOV 659) may be sung to TALLIS' CANON ("All praise to thee, my God, this night," LBW 278).

Maundy Thursday

Where charity and love prevail (TWENTY-FOURTH, LBW 126) may be sung to ST. ANNE ("O God, our help in ages past," LBW 320) or LAND OF REST ("Jerusalem, my happy home," LBW 331).

Good Friday

Were you there (WERE YOU THERE) is at LBW 92.

The Vigil of Easter

We know that Christ (ENGLEBERG) is at LBW 189.

Easter

Now the green blade rises (NOEL NOUVELET) is at LBW 148.

Summer

Many and great (LAC QUI PARLE) is at WOV 794.

Autumn

Praise and thanksgiving, Father, we offer (BUNESSAN) is at LBW 409.

November

I want to walk as a child of the light (HOUSTON) is at WOV 649.

Acknowledgments

Unless otherwise noted, hymns, prayers, and blessings that are published in this collection are copyrighted by Augsburg Fortress Publishers.

Scripture quotations are from the New Revised Standard Version Bible, copyright © 1989 Division of Christian Education of the National Council of Churches of Christ in the United States of America. Used by permission.

Prayers and liturgical texts acknowledged as *LBW* are copyright © 1978 *Lutheran Book of Worship.*

Introduction

I bind unto myself today: Text attributed to Saint Patrick; public domain.

Daily prayer

I bind unto myself today: Text attributed to Saint Patrick; public domain.

I give thanks to you, my heavenly Father: *A Contemporary Translation of Luther's Small Catechism,* tr. Timothy J. Wengert, copyright © 1994 Augsburg Fortress.

O Holy Spirit, enter in: Michael Schirmer; public domain.

You alone are the Holy One: *LBW.*

Send your Holy Spirit: *LBW.*

Almighty God: *LBW.*

Prayer in the Morning

This day God gives me: Text copyright © 1969 Geoffrey Chapman Ltd., administered by Selah Publishing Co., Inc. Used by permission.

Blessed are you, Lord, the God of Israel (Song of Zechariah): The English translation of the Benedictus prepared by the English Language Liturgical Consultation (ELLC), 1988.

As you cause the sun: *Book of Common Worship,* text copyright © 1993 Westminster/John Knox Press. Used by permission.

At midday

Blessed Savior, at this hour: Collect from Noonday Prayer, *Book of Common Prayer* (1979 edition); public domain.

Heavenly Father: *LBW.*

The Lord bless us: *LBW.*

Prayer in the evening

Christ, mighty Savior: Text translation copyright © 1982 United Methodist Publishing House. Used by permission.

My soul proclaims the greatness of the Lord (Song of Mary): The English translation of the Magnificat prepared by the English Language Liturgical Consultation (ELLC), 1988.

Keep watch, dear Lord: Collect from Evening Prayer, *Book of Common Prayer* (1979 edition); public domain.

O God, the life of all who live: Collect from Evening Prayer, *Book of Common Prayer* (1979 edition); public domain.

At bedtime

The Lord almighty: *LBW.*

Into your hands: *LBW.*

Now, Lord, you let your servant go in peace (Song of Simeon): The English translation of the Nunc Dimittis prepared by the English Language Liturgical Consultation (ELLC), 1988.

Visit this house: Collect from Compline, *Book of Common Prayer* (1979 edition); public domain.

I give thanks to you, my heavenly Father: *A Contemporary Translation of Luther's Small Catechism,* tr. Timothy J. Wengert, copyright © 1994 Augsburg Fortress.

The almighty and merciful Lord: *LBW.*

Bedtime prayer with children

All praise to you: *LBW;* public domain.

God, who made the earth and heaven: *LBW;* public domain.

This little light of mine: African American spiritual; public domain.

Children of the heav'nly Father: Text copyright © Board of Publications, Lutheran Church in America.

Sun of my soul: Text by John Keble; public domain.

Thy holy wings: Text by Gracia Grindal, copyright © 1994 Selah Publishing Co., Inc. All rights reserved. Used by permission.

Be near me, Lord Jesus: *LBW;* public domain.

Angel sent by God: public domain.

Jesus Christ, a child so wise: From *Come, Lord Jesus* by Susan Briehl, copyright © 1996 Augsburg Fortress.

Sunday evening

Come, let us join: *LBW;* public domain.

This is the feast: *LBW.*

Jesus Christ is the light: *LBW.*

O Trinity, O blessed Light: Text copyright © 1978 *Lutheran Book of Worship.*

Lord God, whose Son our Savior Jesus Christ: Collect from Evening Prayer, *Book of Common Prayer* (1979 edition); public domain.

The Prayers of Christians

Kyrie, Gloria Patri, Apostles' Creed, Sanctus, The Lord's Prayer, Lamb of God: English translations prepared by the English Language Liturgical Consultation (ELLC), 1988.

Advent

People, look east: Text copyright © 1931 Eleanor Farjeon, administerd by David Higham Associates, Ltd. Used by permission.

O Wisdom, pow'r of God Most High: Altered text copyright © 1997 Augsburg Fortress Publishers.

Christmas

There is no rose of such virtue: Anonymous, 15th century English; public domain.

Angels we have heard on high: public domain.

Epiphany

Arise, your light has come!: Text by Ruth Duck, copyright © 1992 GIA Publications, Inc. All rights reserved. Used by permission.

God of night and of day: From *Catholic Household Blessings and Prayers,* copyright © 1988 United States Catholic Conference. Used by permission.

Lent

O Sun of justice, Jesus Christ: Latin hymn, 6th century; translation copyright © Peter J. Scagnelli. Used by permission.

Lord, have mercy: *LBW.*

Holy God: From Holy Eucharist, *Book of Common Prayer* (1979 edition); public domain.

The Three Days

Where charity and love prevail: public domain.

Holy God, Source of all love: copyright © 1978 *Lutheran Book of Worship* Ministers Desk Edition.

Were you there: African American spiritual; public domain.

Almighty God, your Son: copyright © 1978 *Lutheran Book of Worship* Ministers Desk Edition.